THANE PRINCE'S
QUICK & EASY
SOUPS

···

THANE PRINCE'S
QUICK & EASY
SOUPS

BBC BOOKS

Acknowledgements

No cookery book is ever entirely the work
of the author, so I want to thank all those who helped
encourage and inform me.

Published by BBC Books, a division of
BBC Enterprises Limited, Woodlands,
80 Wood Lane, London W12 0TT

First published 1994
Copyright © Thane Prince 1994
The moral right of the author has been asserted
ISBN 0 563 36949 3

BBC Quick & Easy is a trademark of the
British Broadcasting Corporation

Designed by Judith Robertson
Photographs by Philip Webb
Styling by Philip Webb
Home Economist: Sarah Ramsbottom

Typeset by Goodfellow & Egan Ltd, Cambridge
Printed and bound in Great Britain by Richard Clays Ltd, St Ives plc
Colour separations by Radstock Reproductions Ltd, Midsomer Norton
Cover printed by Richard Clays Ltd, St Ives plc

ABOUT THE AUTHOR

Thane Prince is a lover of good food and a passionate supporter of fresh, seasonal produce but she realizes that life today means there is seldom time to spend laboriously preparing meals. She has a realistic approach to cooking and a firmly held food philosophy – that good food plays a central part in our lives and that a simply prepared meal, shared with family and friends, is one of life's great pleasures.

Thane Prince has been writing for the *Daily Telegraph* and other publications since 1988. In 1990 she was made *Telegraph* Weekend Cook and she also writes a weekly feature for the *Sunday Telegraph*. She is a regular contributor to BBC radio and television and has written four other books: *Quick Cook*, *The Daily Telegraph Book of Cakes, Bakes and Puddings*, *Summer Cook* and *Sainsbury's Quick Cuisine*.

Married with two daughters, she lives in London.

BBC BOOKS' QUICK & EASY COOKERY SERIES

Launched in 1989 by Ken Hom and Sarah Brown, the *Quick & Easy Cookery* series is a culinary winner. Everything about the titles is aimed at quick and easy recipes – the ingredients, the preparation needed and the cooking methods. Eight pages of colour photographs are also included to provide a flash of inspiration for the frantic or faint-hearted.

CONTENTS

INTRODUCTION

There are few things more cheering than a bowl of mulligatawny soup on a cold winter's day or more refreshing than iced gazpacho on a humid summer's evening. Soup has long been a staple dish, internationally enjoyed. Indeed, it is not difficult to imagine that after barbecued mammoth, soup would have been next on the list of culinary evolution.

My love of soups has much to do with the way they can so easily reflect the seasons, using whatever is freshest and best. Almost any vegetable can be made into a soup, though some of the milder ones such as cauliflower need a little help and judicious seasoning.

Little special equipment is needed when making soup, though a large, heavy bottomed saucepan is invaluable. Some recipes in this book use a liquidizer or food processor to reduce the soup to a purée. If you don't have one just omit this step, these soups will still taste good.

Soups vary in character, the most elegant are suitable for serving at the smartest formal dinner party and the chunkier farmhouse soups are perfect for winter picnics or informal one-course meals when served with crusty bread and cheese.

Meal-in-a-bowl soups especially please me as they are economical to make and easy to eat, thus everyone is happy. And the endless variety of soups makes them the perfect fall back meal. A few tins from the store-cupboard, a smoked sausage or some dry-cured bacon and a treat awaits.

Don't use the soup pot as a dustbin, your ingredients must be of top quality if you wish the finished soup to have strong clear flavours.

Home-made soup is a far cry from its tinned cousin. It is delicious, sustaining and economical, easily made from ready-to-hand ingredients, it is quick to prepare and can be left to simmer or chill until needed. Is it any wonder that soup is so popular?

NOTES ON THE RECIPES

Use either metric or imperial measures for the recipes, rather than a mixture of both.

Eggs are size 2.

Spoon measures are level unless otherwise specified.

Where a particular type of stock is not specified choose according to preference or availability.

SOUP STORE-CUPBOARD

I have always found a well-stocked store-cupboard an invaluable asset. It's not just that I'm disorganized, though that is one factor, I find that often there are more people to eat at my table than expected or worse still I have completely forgotten that I have a family to feed, so busily have I been working.

I keep a variety of tinned and dried goods and a goodly number of sauces and seasonings. Do store food in a cool dark place. Light and warmth should be reserved for pets and children.

DASHI

Dashi is a Japanese soup base made from dried bonito tuna. It makes a very good base for fish soups and can be found in oriental markets or health food shops. Usually sold as a powder, it reconstitutes very easily. Don't be put off by the rather fishy smell, it tastes very good.

FLOUR

Possibly the most unfashionable ingredient in these post-*nouvelle cuisine* days, flour is, and always was, a good way of thickening some soups. It must be used carefully and fully cooked before serving and should never be more than vaguely discernible in the velvety texture of the chosen soup.

FROZEN FOODS

I find it helpful to keep a small supply of frozen vegetables such as peas, corn and spinach in the freezer for soup making. White fish fillets such as cod, haddock or hake, frozen prawns and bags of mixed prepared mussels, squid and other shellfish are useful standbys.

When using frozen fish or vegetables in soups it is usually not necessary to alter the cooking times.

HERBS AND SPICES

Most dried herbs aren't worth buying as the flavour is so far removed from the fresh that it is often better not to use them. The exceptions are freeze-dried herbs such as tarragon and thyme, and dried sage and bay leaves. Fortunately these days, due to the wonders of the global food market, fresh herbs are usually easy to find.

Buy whole nutmeg and grate when needed. When possible buy other spices whole, grinding them just before use. If you have to buy spices ground, buy in the smallest possible quantity from a shop with a good turnover.

OLIVE OIL

Apart from recipes where olive oil is used as an added seasoning (as with some of the Italian soups in the book), I would use a good quality French or Spanish oil rather than an expensive extra virgin Tuscan oil. The merit of these costly oils is that they have been made from the first cold pressing of the olives and so have never been heated. To boil them might be viewed as sacrilege.

PASSATA

Passata, usually sold in glass jars or tetrapacks is essentially sieved tomatoes. The purée is not concentrated so the flavour is very fresh and clean. I use it often as a base for soups.

PASTA AND RICE

Adding pasta or rice to a soup gives it bulk. I like to use good quality Italian dried pasta and keep a variety of shapes in the cupboard. Don't worry though if you can't find these packets of miniature soup pasta, broken spaghetti is just as good.

Basmati and long grain rice are the two most suitable for soups. They absorb the flavour of the stock and cook relatively quickly.

PULSES

One surprising fact about pulses is that they don't keep indefinitely. Just because they sit there on the shelf looking for all the world much as they did when you bought them doesn't mean they will cook well. In fact if you have ever had trouble getting dried pulses to soften it will almost certainly be because they were old stock. Buy in small quantities and use up quickly.

I keep red lentils, green lentils and yellow split peas for soup making.

SAUCES AND SEASONINGS

I keep Worcestershire sauce, naturally brewed Japanese soy sauce and Tabasco chilli sauce as I have found all of these to be consistent in taste and quality. And a jar or two of red and green pesto can be useful to spoon into soups at the last moment.

I always use Maldon sea salt crystals and freshly ground black pepper. Ready-ground pepper is little better than talcum powder a few weeks after opening. Purists will insist that white pepper should be used in pale and cream soups but I like the taste of black pepper and don't find it looks offensive, no matter how elegant the recipe. After all I'm the one doing the eating so I use what I enjoy.

As additional seasonings I also keep chilli oil, sesame oil, a selection of vinegars and mustards and a few jars of oriental seasoning such as oyster sauce, hoisin sauce and Thai fish sauce (*nam prik*). These all store well and can be bought either at an oriental food shop or on the specialist food counters in local supermarkets. There is an ever-increasing range of such seasonings so keep checking the shelves.

STOCK

I keep a store of stock cubes made without MSG (monosodium glutamate) to use when I feel the soup needs a more pronounced flavour. Always reconstitute the cube before stirring it into the soup, preferably simmering the stock with some vegetable trimmings and fresh herbs.

Home-made or chill fresh stock keeps very well frozen in small batches and is quick to thaw in either a microwave or in a saucepan over a low heat.

TINS

Choose good quality vegetables for soup: Italian chopped tomatoes in tomato juice are invaluable as are tins of ready-cooked pulses. I keep tinned chick peas, butter beans, red kidney beans and barlotti beans.

I also usually have a tin or two of sweetcorn and one of new potatoes which, at a pinch, can add bulk and substance to a meaty soup.

STOCKS, BROTHS AND CLEAR SOUPS

The word stock seems to take on almost mystical properties when mentioned in cookbooks. Some writers insist that one must only use home-made stock, others mention supposedly halcyon days when pots bubbled on the back of kitchen ranges. Stock, they seem to say, not only sorts the good from the bad but is the elixir of life and the key to inner happiness. All very well but we are talking about flavoured water here and as with most foods there can be bad stock quite as easily as good stock. To my mind the stock pot of old yielded a broth that tasted more of the dustbin than anything else, for how can the flavour be fresh and true when a rag-bag of ingredients are used? The same applies to fresh stock made in the kitchen, should you use tired soggy veg the stock will be equally weary.

If you don't have sufficient time to make a good fresh stock from good fresh ingredients then it is best to use plain water which at least will add nothing harmful to the flavours of your dish. You can also use fresh stock bought from a supermarket chill cabinet or even a stock cube.

Yes, I did say stock cube, but you must take care when using them. Try to buy cubes that don't contain monosodium glutamate. A new brand is becoming widely available in supermarkets or check out your local health food shop.

Always prepare the cube separately: place the crumbled cube with about a third as much water again as it says on the packet into a saucepan and simmer for a few minutes with, if possible, some chopped onion, carrot and celery along with a few parsley stalks and a bay leaf to freshen up the flavour. This can be cooking while you prepare the other ingredients for the soup.

CONTENTS

BEEF STOCK

M A K E S

—— approx 1.5 litres (2¹/₂ pints) ——

If you have time at weekends, you can make a good beef stock to use in robustly flavoured soups such as *French onion* (see p.38) or *Beef broth with tortellini* (see p.25). While making beef stock might, at first, seem much too time-consuming, actually once the stock is simmering it needs little attention. It will keep for three to four days, but also freezes well.

———

Pre-heat the oven to 230°C/450°F/Gas 8.

Place the bones in a large roasting dish. Put the vegetables in a bowl with the oil and toss until they are coated. Empty these onto the bones then place in the oven stirring occasionally until everything is a rich dark brown, about 30 minutes.

Tip the contents of the dish into a large saucepan and add 1.2 litres (2 pints) of water, bring to the boil and skim. Add a further 1.2 (2 pints) of water and simmer over a low heat for 4 hours!

Strain through a fine sieve and taste. If the flavour is too light boil over high heat to reduce.

Cool and refrigerate.

INGREDIENTS

PREPARATION TIME
10 minutes
COOKING TIME
4–5 hours

900 g (2 lb) beef or veal
bones, cut into 5 cm
(2 inch) pieces
1 medium onion, quartered
2 carrots, scrubbed and
chopped
4 sticks celery, roughly
chopped
1 tablespoon light olive oil

CHICKEN STOCK

M A K E S

—— approx 900ml (1¹/₂ pints) ——

INGREDIENTS

PREPARATION TIME
10 minutes
COOKING TIME
35–45 minutes

Chicken bones/carcass or
  2 chicken thighs
2 tablespoons light olive oil
1 medium onion, chopped
2 carrots, scrubbed and
  chopped
2 sticks celery, chopped
2 mushrooms, chopped
A few parsley stalks, chopped
2 bay leaves
Sea salt and freshly ground
  black pepper

Again a recipe for weekends, good chicken stock can be made from chicken bones or the carcass of a roast chicken. Don't boil the bones for more than about 40 minutes or the stock will start to taste sour. Don't skimp on the time it takes to fry the bones and vegetables, much of the flavour and colour of the finished stock comes from this caramelization process.

Roughly chop up the chicken bones, carcass or thighs. Heat the oil in a heavy pan and fry them until they colour slightly. Add the chopped vegetables and fry these too until they are pale golden brown in colour.

Add the herbs, season with salt and pepper and add 1.2 litres (2 pints) water to cover the solids in the pan. Simmer over a low heat, topping up with water as necessary, for 30–40 minutes.

Strain through a fine sieve and taste the stock. If it is too strong dilute with a little water. If the flavour is not concentrated enough boil over a high heat to reduce.

Cool and store in the fridge until needed. Fresh stock keeps for 3–4 days.

VEGETABLE STOCK

MAKES

—— 1.2 litres (2 pints) ——

A simple vegetable stock will add extra flavour to soups and is also excellent to use when making risottos and sauces, plus a huge variety of vegetarian dishes.

Heat the oil in a heavy saucepan and sweat the onion and leek until soft and transparent. Add the garlic and cook for a further minute. Now add the remaining vegetables, herbs, a good pinch of salt and some pepper. Cook for a further 2 minutes before covering with 1.75 litres (3 pints) of water and simmering for 20 minutes. Strain through a fine sieve pressing the solids well to extract as much flavour as possible.

This stock keeps for 2–3 days in the fridge and also freezes well. Put into small batches for easy use.

INGREDIENTS

PREPARATION TIME
10 minutes
COOKING TIME
25–35 minutes

1–2 tablespoons light
vegetable oil
1 onion, finely chopped
1 leek, cleaned and chopped
1–2 garlic cloves, chopped
2 sticks celery, finely chopped
2 carrots, scrubbed and
chopped
2 mushrooms, chopped
2 tomatoes, chopped
2–3 stems each, parsley,
thyme and bay leaves
Sea salt and freshly ground
black pepper

FISH STOCK

MAKES

—— approx 1.2 litres (2 pints) ——

PREPARATION TIME
5 minutes
COOKING TIME
25–35 minutes

900 g (2 lb) white fish bones
25 g (1 oz) unsalted butter
1 leek, cleaned and chopped
1 onion, chopped
1 stick celery, chopped
120 ml (4 fl oz) white wine
Whole black peppercorns
A few parsley stalks

Fish stock is by far the quickest stock to make. Ask your fishmonger for as many white fish bones, especially those of flat fish such as sole, turbot or halibut, as he can spare. To avoid giving a bitter taint to the stock, wash the bones well to remove any traces of blood.

Wash the bones very well, removing all traces of blood, then chop them roughly.

Melt the butter in a large saucepan and cook the vegetables over a moderate heat until they soften. Don't let them colour. Now add the fish bones and cook these, stirring often, until they loose their raw smell, about 3–4 minutes. Once the bones are cooked add the white wine a few peppercorns and the parsley stalks.

Cover the bones with 1.75 litres (3 pints) of water and simmer for 20–30 minutes. Strain through a fine sieve.

Reduce the stock by boiling to give the required strength. This stock keeps for 2 days in the fridge and freezes well.

SHERRIED MUSHROOM CONSOMMÉ

S E R V E S
—— 4 ——

This elegant soup has very finely sliced mushrooms and a dash of dry sherry added at the last moment to enhance the flavours.

———

Bring the stock to the boil in a large saucepan and add the shallot, garlic, celery, carrot, and minced beef. Skim any scum that rises to the surface.

Simmer for 5 minutes then strain through a fine sieve lined with muslin or kitchen paper.

Pour the stock back into a clean saucepan and re-heat. Finely slice the button mushrooms and add to the soup.

Simmer for 2 minutes then add the sherry, taste and adjust the seasoning. Serve hot.

INGREDIENTS

PREPARATION TIME
10 minutes
COOKING TIME
15 minutes

900 ml (1¹/₂ pints) beef stock
1 shallot, chopped
1 garlic clove, crushed
2 sticks celery, chopped
2 carrots, peeled and chopped
100 g (4 oz) lean minced beef
100 g (4 oz) button mushrooms
2–3 tablespoons medium-dry sherry
Sea salt and freshly ground black pepper

HOT AND SOUR SOUP

SERVES
—— 4 ——

INGREDIENTS

PREPARATION TIME
10 minutes
COOKING TIME
10 minutes

1.2 litres (2 pints) vegetable
  or chicken stock
1 teaspoon Thai fish sauce
  (nam prik)
2.5 cm (1 inch) piece lemon
  grass, finely chopped
3 lime leaves, roughly torn
2 tablespoons light soy sauce
1 teaspoon caster sugar
2 tablespoons fresh lemon or
  lime juice
50 g (2 oz) oyster or button
  mushrooms, sliced
1–2 small green fresh chillies,
  de-seeded and chopped
Fresh coriander leaves to
  garnish

Hot and sour soups are popular throughout the Far East. This one comes from Thailand and is wonderfully versatile. You can add chunks of chicken breast, raw prawns, small slivers of pork or white crabmeat to the base recipe. Thai fish sauce (*nam prik*), lime leaves or zest, chillies and lemon grass are available from many supermarkets or oriental grocers. When using lemon grass choose the thick fleshy end. Do take care when preparing chillies. Wear rubber gloves and wash your hands well after chopping. The oil from chillies is very hot and can be painful if you touch your eyes with unwashed fingers.

In a large saucepan heat the stock. If you are using chicken add it now. Simmer for 1–2 minutes. Stir in the remaining ingredients and cook until the mushrooms are just tender, about 3–4 minutes. If you are using fish or shellfish add this now and simmer for 1 minute to cook through.

Pour into warm bowls and garnish with fresh coriander leaves.

LAKSA SOUP

S E R V E S

—— 4 ——

Laksa soup comes from Indonesia but has become almost a national dish in Australia where I first tasted it. The wonderful variety of fresh ingredients available and the multi-ethnic influences in cooking are fast making Australia a centre for fine food. This soup makes a meal-in-a-bowl.

Soak the noodles in boiling water for 4–5 minutes. In a large saucepan brown the onion in the oil and add the *tom yum* paste. Cook for 1 minute.

Add the stock, lemon grass, lime leaves or zest, half the coriander and the lemon or lime juice. Crumble in the creamed coconut and stir until it dissolves. Add the fish sauce, chicken slices and the drained noodles. Simmer for 2 minutes then add the prawns and heat through.

Serve in hot bowls garnished with the remaining coriander and spring onions.

INGREDIENTS

PREPARATION TIME
10 minutes
COOKING TIME
10 minutes

225 g (8 oz) Chinese-style egg noodles
1 small onion, sliced
1 tablespoon vegetable oil
1 tablespoon tom yum *paste or Thai red curry paste*
1.2 litres (2 pints) chicken stock
10 cm (4 in) piece lemon grass, chopped
4 lime leaves, roughly torn or lime zest
A handful of fresh coriander, chopped
Juice of lemon or a large lime
100 g (4 oz) block of creamed coconut
1 tablespoon Thai fish sauce (nam prik)
2 boned, skinless chicken breasts, finely sliced
100 g (4 oz) raw peeled prawns
3 spring onions, chopped
100 g (4 oz) fresh beansprouts

JAPANESE-STYLE NOODLE SOUP

SERVES
—— 4 ——

PREPARATION TIME
10 minutes
COOKING TIME
10 minutes

*350 g (12 oz) Udon, soba or
plain wheat flour noodles,
or tagliatelle*
*900 ml (1¹/₂ pints) instant
dashi stock*
1 tablespoon mirin
teaspoon soft brown sugar
*1 tablespoon Japanese or light
soy sauce*
*8 shiitake mushrooms, finely
sliced*
*A good handful of fresh
spinach leaves*
4 spring onions, sliced

If you can't gather all the ingredients for this dish do make inspired substitutions! Chicken stock for dashi (see p. 11), sweet sherry for mirin (rice wine) and field mushrooms for shiitake. Health food shops are a good source of noodles, Japanese soy sauce and instant stock.

Bring a large pan of water to the boil and cook the noodles for 4–5 minutes. Drain and refresh in a bowl of cold water.

Heat the stock and add the mirin, brown sugar and soy sauce. Put in the mushrooms and simmer for 2–3 minutes.

Add the drained noodles and spinach and re-heat until everything is hot. Spoon into bowls and serve scattered with the spring onions.

Cubes of tofu, small pieces of chicken, crab sticks or prawns can be added to this basic recipe.

BEEF BROTH WITH TORTELLINI

SERVES
— 4 —

This is one of the simpler soups from Italy and makes a good beginning to an Italian meal. Buy the tortellini ready made either fresh or in packets from the dried pasta section of the supermarket.

———

Bring the stock to a boil in a large pan. Add the tortellini and simmer until the pasta is cooked to taste, about 7–8 minutes for fresh pasta and 15–17 minutes for dried depending on size. If the stock reduces too much during cooking add water.

Add the shredded ham and season to taste. Serve in warm soup bowls with lots of freshly grated parmesan cheese.

INGREDIENTS

PREPARATION TIME
5 minutes
COOKING TIME
10–20 minutes

1.2 litres (2 pints) beef stock
175 g (6 oz) dried tortellini
or 340 g 12 oz fresh
tortellini
50 g (2 oz) lean finely sliced
ham, shredded
Salt and pepper
Freshly grated parmesan
cheese

PENNSYLVANIA-STYLE CHICKEN NOODLE SOUP

S E R V E S

—— 4 ——

Chicken noodle soups may have been debased by the awfulness of the packet mix but in Pennsylvania the early German immigrants began a long tradition of wonderful noodle soups full of thick egg noodles and chunks of farm-raised chicken.

Bring a large pan of lightly salted water to the boil and cook the noodles for 5 minutes. Drain.

Heat the chicken stock in a large pan, add the bay leaves and vegetables. Simmer for 5 minutes.

Dice the chicken breasts and add to the soup with the noodles. Simmer gently until the noodles are cooked through. Taste and adjust the seasoning, there should be plenty of pepper. Serve at once in hot bowls scattered with the parsley.

INGREDIENTS

PREPARATION TIME
10 minutes
COOKING TIME
15 minutes

225 g (8 oz) egg noodles (the fatter the better)
1.2 litres (2 pints) chicken stock
2 bay leaves
3 medium carrots, peeled and sliced
2 leeks, cleaned and sliced
2–3 sticks celery, sliced
2 large boned, skinless chicken breasts
Sea salt and freshly ground black pepper
Chopped flat leaf parsley to garnish

SIMPLE CRAB SOUP

S E R V E S
—— 4 ——

Shellfish soups are delicious. A simple stock can be made by lightly crushing the shells and simmering with a few seasoning vegetables. Use a ready-dressed crab, packed in its shell for this recipe – they are available from fishmongers and supermarkets.

Scrape the crabmeat from the shell and reserve. Now crush the shell roughly using a rolling-pin and place in a saucepan with the oil and a tablespoon of each of the chopped vegetables. Cook, stirring, for 2–3 minutes then add the water.

Simmer for 5 minutes before straining through a fine sieve. Return the stock to a clean saucepan, add the remaining vegetables, tomato purée, wine and seasoning and simmer for 10 minutes. Stir in the crabmeat and cream. Reheat and adjust the seasoning.

Serve in warm bowls garnished with the chives.

INGREDIENTS

PREPARATION TIME
10 minutes
COOKING TIME
20 minutes

1 medium crab, ready-dressed
  in shell, thawed if frozen
1 tablespoon light
  vegetable oil
2 carrots, peeled and very
  finely diced
2 sticks celery, finely diced
2 shallots, finely diced
900 ml (1½ pints) water
1 teaspoon tomato purée
120 ml (4 fl oz) white wine
Sea salt and freshly ground
  black pepper
150 ml (5 fl oz) single cream
Finely chopped chives
  to garnish

CHINESE WONTON SOUP

SERVES

—— 4 ——

Ready-made wontons are available, frozen, from oriental supermarkets. You can also buy Chinese greens and soy sauce at very reasonable prices. Serve the soup with prawn crackers, again easily available ready made.

Bring the stock to the boil in a large saucepan and simmer the wontons for 3–4 minutes. Add the remaining ingredients and cook for a further 2–3 minutes. Serve hot.

INGREDIENTS

PREPARATION TIME
10 minutes
COOKING TIME
10 minutes

*900 ml (1¹/₂ pints) chicken
stock
16 ready-made wontons,
thawed
1–2 tablespoons soy sauce
teaspoon sesame oil
100 g (4 oz) shredded
Chinese leaves or spinach
4 spring onions, shredded*

CHILLIED CHICKEN CONSOMMÉ

SERVES

—— 4 ——

The first spoonful of this fiery soup is bound to send a variety of sensations through you. I first tried it on a visit to Mexico and was simultaneously startled by the heat of the chillies and captivated by the wonderfully rich flavours of the stock and green coriander.

Bring the stock to simmering point in a large saucepan. Finely chop the chicken and add to the stock. Chop the coriander and reserve.

Wearing gloves, de-seed the chillies and chop them finely. Add to the soup and simmer for 2 minutes. Now add the coriander and cook for a further 2 minutes. Taste and adjust the seasoning, then serve at once.

INGREDIENTS

PREPARATION TIME
10 minutes
COOKING TIME
10 minutes

*900 ml (1¹/₂ pints)
concentrated chicken stock
1 boned, skinless chicken
breast fillet
1–2 small green fresh chillies
A good handful of fresh
coriander leaves
Sea salt and freshly ground
black pepper*

VEGETABLE SOUPS

Vegetable soups can be as simple or as sophisticated as you please. They have the distinct advantage of being easy to make and the combinations can be decided by using whatever veg you have in the fridge.

Most of the soups given in this chapter are made using water in place of stock as this allows the flavour of the vegetables to be dominant. This having been said, you must use good quality, fresh ingredients. Vegetables past their prime – tired greens and limp carrots – will yield a soup equally lacking in vitality.

Prepare the vegetables just before use: always wash leeks and leaf vegetables carefully to remove any grit or pesticide residue and peel or pare others as finely as possible.

CONTENTS

QUICK MINESTRONE

S E R V E S
—— 4 ——

Perhaps the most famous of all Italian soups is mine-strone, a classic vegetable and pasta soup that has a bacon-flavoured stock and is often made so thick you can 'slice' it.

Place the bacon in a deep saucepan and cook until the fat melts. Add the oil, onion and garlic and cook, stirring often, until the onion softens.

Now add the carrots, celery and drained beans and mix well. Add the tomatoes and macaroni, pour in the water and season well. Bring to the boil and simmer for 15 minutes.

Meanwhile finely slice the cabbage and the courgettes and add along with the peas.

Simmer for a further 15 minutes then serve into warm bowls garnished with basil and Parmesan.

INGREDIENTS

PREPARATION TIME
15 minutes
COOKING TIME
35 minutes

100 g (4 oz) bacon, chopped
2 tablespoons olive oil
1 large onion, chopped
1 plump garlic clove, chopped
3 carrots, peeled and thinly
 sliced
3 sticks celery, sliced
1 × 400 g (14 oz) tin haricot
 beans, drained
1 × 200 g (7 oz) tin chopped
 Italian tomatoes
100 g (4 oz) quick-cook
 macaroni
1.2 litres (2 pints) water
Sea salt and freshly ground
 black pepper
1 small white cabbage
4 medium courgettes
100 g (4 oz) frozen peas
Fresh basil leaves to garnish
Freshly grated Parmesan to
 garnish

BROAD BEAN AND SUMMER HERB SOUP

S E R V E S
—— 4 ——

INGREDIENTS

PREPARATION TIME
5 minutes + 5 minutes sieving
COOKING TIME
10 minutes

50 g (2 oz) butter
100 g (4 oz) chopped onion
450 g (1 lb) fresh or frozen broad beans (shelled weight)
2 teaspoons fresh thyme or savory, or 1 teaspoon dried herbes de Provence
Sea salt and freshly ground black pepper
900 ml (1¹/₂ pints) boiling water

Philip Britten of the Capital Hotel in London first showed me how to make this simple soup. Make it in summer with seasonal beans and herbs. At other times you can use frozen broad beans and whatever fresh herb is available. This soup can be garnished with a few shelled beans, some soured cream or a few chopped chives.

Melt the butter in a large saucepan and cook the onion over a low heat until transparent.

Add the broad beans and herbs and toss them in the butter. Season well and pour on the boiling water. Boil for 4–5 minutes then purée and pass through a sieve.

Re-heat and adjust the seasoning.

Opposite: BROAD BEAN AND SUMMER HERB SOUP
BEEF BROTH WITH TORTELLINI *(Page 25)*

CABBAGE AND BACON SOUP WITH CHEESE DUMPLINGS

S E R V E S
—— 4 ——

A hearty soup this, ideal after a long walk or on Bonfire Night. When I made this for my sister she was astonished that it took so little time and effort to prepare.

In a large saucepan brown the bacon in the oil. Add the potato cubes and stir well. Now add the carrots, onion, caraway seeds and a little salt and pepper.

Fry everything together for a few minutes then add the water and bring to the boil. Simmer for about 10 minutes or until the vegetables are almost cooked.

Meanwhile make the dumplings: sift the flour with the baking powder and rub in the butter. Add the herbs and cheese and mix to a stiff paste with the milk.

Keep the soup at a rolling boil and put in the cabbage. Now place spoonfuls of the dumpling mixture into the pan and press them gently under the surface of the soup. Don't worry if the pan looks rather full at this stage as this is a very chunky soup.

Half cover the pan and simmer for 4–5 minutes.

Taste and adjust the seasoning, then serve at once.

INGREDIENTS

PREPARATION TIME
15 minutes
COOKING TIME
20–25 minutes

100 g (4 oz) streaky bacon
1 tablespoon olive oil
350 g (12 oz) potatoes,
  cubed (peeled weight)
2 medium carrots peeled and
  sliced
1 medium onion, chopped
1 teaspoon caraway seeds
Sea salt and freshly ground
  black pepper
1.2 litres (2 pints) water
$^1/_2$ savoy or green cabbage,
  roughly sliced

FOR THE DUMPLINGS
100 g (4 oz) plain flour
1 teaspoon baking powder
25 g (1 oz) butter
1 teaspoon freeze-dried mixed
  herbs
50 g (2 oz) hard cheese,
  grated
3 tablespoons milk

Opposite: CABBAGE AND BACON SOUP WITH CHEESE DUMPLINGS
TOMATO AND TARRAGON SOUP *(Page 61)*

CALDO VERDE

S E R V E S

—— 4 ——

PREPARATION TIME
15 minutes
COOKING TIME
30 minutes

2 large onions, finely chopped
4 tablespoons olive oil
2 garlic cloves, crushed
900 g (2 lb) potatoes, peeled
    and diced
1 medium savoy or green
    cabbage, finely sliced
1.2 litres (2 pints) water
Sea salt and freshly ground
    black pepper
450 g (1 lb) fresh spinach,
    washed
A small bunch of spring
    onions, chopped
Lemon juice or wine vinegar
    to taste

This Portuguese potato and cabbage soup has many different recipes but essentially it is a thick vegetarian soup, made to feed hungry farm workers, with easily available cheap ingredients. Like many such rustic dishes it is delicious. Kale is a good alternative to cabbage, fresh spinach is added at the last minute along with chopped spring onions. The flavour is lifted by the addition of a little lemon juice or wine vinegar.

In a large saucepan fry the onions in the oil until they start to brown, then add the garlic and fry until this too colours.

Add the potatoes, cabbage and water and season well. Simmer for about 20 minutes, mash the potatoes roughly with a fork then add the spinach and spring onions and cook for 5 minutes. Taste and adjust the seasoning, adding lemon juice or wine vinegar to taste. Extra water may be added if needed as the soup cooks.

CREAMY ONION SOUP

SERVES
—— 4 ——

R ich and creamy, this onion soup is best made with the large, rather sweet onions from Spain. Cook them in butter and then season this rich soup with lots of freshly ground black pepper.

In a large saucepan heat the butter and oil. Add the chopped onion and cook until soft and transparent, about 5 minutes.

Stir in the flour and then add the milk a little at a time until you have a creamy sauce. Thin this with half the water, season with salt and pepper and simmer for 10 minutes. Taste the soup, adding extra seasoning or thinning with water as necessary. Serve with the croûtons and garnished with chopped parsley.

INGREDIENTS

PREPARATION TIME
10 minutes
COOKING TIME
15 minutes

25 g (1 oz) butter
1 tablespoon vegetable oil
750 g (1¹/₂ lb) Spanish onions, chopped
2 tablespoons plain flour
600 ml (1 pint) semi-skimmed milk
600 ml (1 pint) water
Sea salt and freshly ground black pepper
Chopped fresh parsley to garnish
Crisp garlic croûtons to serve (see p. 127)

FRENCH ONION SOUP

S E R V E S
—— 4 ——

PREPARATION TIME
10 minutes
COOKING TIME
50 minutes

2 tablespoons butter
1 tablespoon oil
1 kg (2¹/₄ lb) onions, thinly
   sliced
1 heaped teaspoon granulated
   sugar
1.2 litres (2 pints) well-
   flavoured stock (beef is
   best)
Sea salt and freshly ground
   black pepper
TO SERVE
Thin slices of French bread
Dijon mustard
Grated Gruyère

It is said that the ultra chic of Paris society used to flock to Les Halles, the Paris vegetable market, to drink this soup after late nights of revelry. They would sit in cafés, alongside the market traders, warming themselves with the rich onion-flavoured broth and chewing on the cheese-encrusted bread. Here I have to admit that the onions must be fried slowly to give a rich full flavour, so this soup is not quick, but it is easy!

In a heavy-bottomed pan melt the butter with the oil and cook the onions, partially covered, over a low heat for 30 minutes. Stir occasionally. The onions should be very soft but not coloured at this stage.

Now add the sugar and turn up the heat. Brown the onions, stirring constantly. When the mixture is a light golden brown add the stock, season lightly and simmer for 20 minutes.

Toast the bread on both sides and spread one side of each piece with mustard. Pile some cheese onto each piece. Heat the grill and, having spooned the soup into warm, heatproof bowls, float 2 or 3 cheese-topped rounds of bread on top of each. Flash under the grill to melt the cheese.

Take care when eating this soup – it is very hot!

TOURAIN BLANCHI À L'AIL

S E R V E S

—— 4 ——

It is said in the Dordogne region of France that the only part of the duck that is not eaten is its quack and this recipe for a simple peasant soup shows how even the fat is used for flavouring this garlic soup. Goose or duck fat is ideal if you happen to have some, otherwise use dripping or even olive oil. Fresh plump cloves of garlic have a pleasant, sweet flavour, best for this recipe.

Finely slice the onions and garlic. Melt the fat or dripping in a large saucepan and fry the sliced vegetables until they are soft but not coloured.

Stir in the flour, mixing well, and cook for 2 minutes before adding the water or stock. Season with salt and pepper and simmer for 30 minutes.

Beat the egg yolks with the vinegar and, having removed the soup from the heat, mix this in. The soup will thicken slightly. Place the bread in a warmed tureen and spoon over the soup. Serve at once.

INGREDIENTS

PREPARATION TIME
10 minutes
COOKING TIME
40 minutes

225 g (8 oz) onions, sliced
100 g (4 oz) plump fresh
    cloves garlic, sliced
2 tablespoons goose fat or
    dripping
1 heaped tablespoon plain
    flour
1 litre (1³/₄ pints) water or
    stock
Sea salt and freshly ground
    black pepper
2 egg yolks
1 tablespoon wine vinegar
6 thick slices country-style
    white bread

LEEK AND POTATO SOUP

SERVES

—— 4 ——

In the repertoire of classic soups leek and potato rates very highly. Smooth, pale and creamy this soup should have a delicate but definite flavour. Made ahead and chilled it can also be served cold when it is called Vichyssoise. Should you wish to serve this soup chilled use 1–2 tablespoons of light vegetable oil in place of the butter to give a better texture.

INGREDIENTS

PREPARATION TIME
10 minutes
COOKING TIME
25 minutes

75 g (1¹/₂ lb) floury potatoes,
peeled
450 g (1 lb) leeks, cleaned
50 g (2 oz) butter
900 ml (1¹/₂ pints) light
chicken or vegetable stock
or water
Sea salt and freshly ground
black pepper
150 ml (5 fl oz) single cream
Chopped fresh chives
to garnish

Cut the potatoes into even-sized chunks. Slice the leeks. (If you want pale soup use only the white part of the leeks, otherwise use the green too.)

Melt the butter in a large pan and carefully sweat the leeks for 5 minutes. Do not let them catch and colour. Add the potatoes and stir well, coating the vegetables in the butter.

Add the stock or water, season and bring to the boil. Simmer for 10–15 minutes or until the potatoes are soft.

Liquidize in small batches until smooth then return to the pan. Stir in the cream and bring to boiling point. Serve scattered with the chives.

CELERIAC AND BACON SOUP

S E R V E S

—— 4 ——

Celeriac is a rather strange-looking vegetable whose tough, raw root belies the smooth texture and delicate flavour. A very versatile vegetable, celeriac cooks to give a delicious smooth purée that marries well with potato as a topping for fish or shepherd's pie and tastes wonderful when mixed with bacon as in this hearty, warming soup.

Heat the oil in a deep saucepan and fry the bacon pieces until crisp. Remove, leaving as much fat in the pan as possible, and reserve.

Fry the onion until soft, then add the celeriac and potatoes. Toss everything well in the hot fat then add the water, thyme and seasoning.

Bring to the boil and simmer until the vegetables are soft, about 10–15 minutes. Purée in batches, adding the cream, if used, and parsley to the last batch.

Re-heat. If the soup is too thick, thin with a little milk, taste and adjust the seasoning.

Serve hot, garnished with the bacon pieces.

INGREDIENTS

PREPARATION TIME
15 minutes
COOKING TIME
25 minutes

1 tablespoon oil
175 g (6 oz) rindless streaky
    bacon, chopped
1 medium onion, chopped
750 g (1¹/₂ lb) celeriac, peeled
    and cubed
2 medium potatoes, peeled
    and cubed
1.2 litres (2 pints) water
¹/₄ teaspoon freeze-dried
    thyme
Sea salt and freshly ground
    black pepper
150 ml (5 fl oz) single cream
    (optional)
2 tablespoons chopped
    fresh parsley

BUTTER BEAN AND CARROT SOUP

SERVES
—— 4 ——

PREPARATION TIME
15 minutes
COOKING TIME
25 minutes

6–8 sun-dried tomato halves,
  sliced
2 tablespoons olive oil
1 large onion, chopped
2 garlic cloves, crushed
3 medium carrots, peeled
  and sliced
3 sticks celery, sliced
900 ml (1½ pints) water
1 × 400 g (14 oz) tin butter
  beans, drained
½ teaspoon crushed fresh
  thyme leaves
Freshly ground black pepper
1 tablespoon balsamic
  or wine vinegar

There is an old joke in my family that is wheeled out every time I serve this soup. It goes something like this: 'What's for supper?'

'Bean soup.'

'It may have been soup, but what is it now.' Exit with roars of laughter!

This is very unfair to what is a delicious and nutritious meal. Here I have used tinned butter beans but by all means cook dried beans ahead if you have time.

———

Place the sun-dried tomatoes into a bowl, cover with boiling water and leave to soak.

In a large saucepan heat the oil and fry the onion until soft. Add the garlic and cook for a further minute. Now stir in the carrots and celery. Add the water, butter beans, thyme, drained tomatoes and a few grinds of black pepper.

Simmer the soup for 15–20 minutes then taste and adjust the seasoning. Add enough vinegar to lift the flavour and give the soup a little bite. Serve hot.

CHEDDAR CHEESE AND BROCCOLI SOUP

SERVES

— 4 —

I thought I wouldn't enjoy cheese soups until I tried this one cooked for me by a friend from North Carolina. We have a distinct advantage when making this soup in Britain as the Cheddar available here has a much tangier flavour.

Frozen broccoli can be used – cook it according to the instructions on the packet, drain and chop before adding to the soup.

———

Cut the broccoli into small pieces and blanch in boiling water for two minutes. Drain and refresh in iced water.

Mix the flour and butter in a deep pan and cook until you have a pale roux. Add the milk a little at a time and beat until you have a smooth sauce the consistency of single cream. Simmer over a low heat for a minute or two until no taste of raw flour remains. Season to taste.

Remove from the heat and allow to cool for a few moments before stirring in the cheese, mixing until it dissolves. Add the broccoli and re-heat the soup before serving in warmed bowls accompanied by hot bread.

INGREDIENTS

PREPARATION TIME
10 minutes
COOKING TIME
10 minutes

225 g (8 oz) broccoli florets
25 g (1 oz) plain flour
25 g (1 oz) butter
1.2 litres (2 pints) semi-skimmed milk
Sea salt and freshly ground black pepper.
225 g (8 oz) mature Cheddar, grated

STILTON AND CELERY SOUP

SERVES
—— 4 ——

If you have some rather dry Stilton cheese left over at Christmas along with a head of celery, you can make a rich cheese soup that has a distinctly British flavour.

Before chopping the celery, cut off any tough strings to improve the finished texture of the soup.

Melt the butter and cook the celery and shallots until soft. Stir in the flour and mix well.

Add a little milk, beating constantly. Gradually add the remaining milk and simmer for 5 minutes.

Now stir in the Stilton and season to taste. Keep the soup over a low heat until the Stilton has almost melted completely then serve in warm bowls garnished with the chives and chopped walnuts.

INGREDIENTS

PREPARATION TIME
10 minutes
COOKING TIME
10 minutes

50 g (2 oz) butter
225 g (8 oz) celery, sliced
2 shallots, finely chopped
25 g (1 oz) plain flour
1.2 litres (2 pints) semi-
*   skimmed milk*
175 g (6 oz) Stilton,
*   crumbled*
Salt and freshly ground
*   black pepper*
Chopped fresh chives
*   to garnish*
2 tablespoons finely chopped
*   walnuts to garnish*

YELLOW PEPPER SOUP

S E R V E S

—— 4 ——

Not so long ago red and yellow peppers were a rare and exotic vegetable. These days they are readily found, year round, in supermarkets and greengrocers'.

Before making this soup you can grill the peppers and remove the skins and skin the tomatoes, so once liquidized you will not need to sieve it. This takes a little time but saves one step of the recipe below. Or peel the peppers with a sharp knife or potato peeler and substitute tinned chopped tomatoes. The choice is yours.

———

Heat the oil in a large pan and fry the onion until soft. Add the garlic and peppers and cook for 2–3 minutes. Then add the tomatoes and water and season lightly.

Bring the soup to the boil and simmer for 10–15 minutes or until the peppers are very soft.

Liquidize in small batches and then rub through a sieve into a large saucepan. This is not as arduous as it sounds and takes only a couple of minutes. Taste and adjust the seasoning.

Mix the crème fraîche with the chives and serve the soup garnished with a blob of this and a few torn basil leaves.

INGREDIENTS

PREPARATION TIME
15 minutes
COOKING TIME
20 minutes

2 tablespoons olive oil
1 onion, chopped
1 garlic clove, chopped
2 large yellow peppers,
	de-seeded and chopped
6 plump tomatoes, chopped,
	or 200 g (7 oz) tinned
	chopped tomatoes
900 ml (1½ pints water)
Sea salt and freshly ground
	black pepper
2 generous tablespoons
	crème fraîche
1 tablespoon chopped
	fresh chives
Fresh basil leaves to garnish

CURRIED PARSNIP SOUP

SERVES

—— 4 ——

PREPARATION TIME
15 minutes
COOKING TIME
20 minutes

2 tablespoons oil
1 large onion, chopped
1 garlic clove, crushed
4 medium parsnips, peeled
    and diced
1 teaspoon cumin seeds
1 teaspoon ground coriander
$^1/_2$ teaspoon turmeric
1 generous tablespoon mango
    chutney
Sea salt and freshly ground
    black pepper
900 ml (1$^1/_2$ pints) water
A few drops of Tabasco
Juice of $^1/_2$ lemon
Chopped fresh coriander
    to garnish

I read recently that parsnips could be par-boiled before use to remove some of their sweetness and thought how dreadful. For it is precisely because parsnips are so sweet that they make such delightful dishes. I like to add them to gratins as well as roasting them, but best of all I like to mix their sweet/savoury flavour with spices as in this lightly curried soup.

In a large pan heat the oil and fry the onion until soft. Add the garlic and parsnips and cook for a further 2 minutes. Now add the cumin, coriander and turmeric and fry, stirring constantly, for a further minute. Add the chutney, salt, pepper and then the water. Bring to the boil and simmer for 10 minutes or until the vegetables are soft.

Liquidize the soup in small batches and return to the pan. Taste the soup adding Tabasco and lemon juice to sharpen the flavour.

Serve sprinkled with the fresh coriander.

BROWN-CAP MUSHROOM AND BROWN BREAD SOUP

SERVES
—— 4 ——

Brown-cap mushrooms are a newer addition to the vegetable shelves than button mushrooms. I like them because they are full-flavoured and nutty tasting. This soup is thickened with brown bread, a traditional way to thicken a soup that is both quick and easy. Use a wholemeal brown loaf for extra goodness.

In a large pan fry the onion in the butter until soft. Chop the mushrooms coarsely and add to the pan. Season well and cook for 2 minutes. Add the stock and bring to the boil. Simmer for 10–15 minutes, then liquidize in batches.

Return to a clean pan and thicken with breadcrumbs. Add the sherry, freshly chopped tarragon and taste. Adjust seasoning and serve, topping each bowl with a swirl of single cream.

INGREDIENTS

PREPARATION TIME
10 minutes
COOKING TIME
20 minutes

1 medium onion, finely
  chopped
1 tablespoon butter
450 g (1 lb) Brown-cap
  mushrooms
900 ml (1½ pints) vegetable
  or chicken stock
Sea salt and freshly ground
  black pepper
About 50 g (2 oz) 3-day-old
  brown breadcrumbs
2–3 tablespoons dry sherry
Single cream to garnish
2 tablespoons fresh tarragon,
  chopped

LETTUCE AND MINT SOUP

S E R V E S

—— 4 ——

PREPARATION TIME
15 minutes
COOKING TIME
20 minutes

25 g (1 oz) butter
1 onion, finely chopped
2 medium potatoes, peeled
   and diced
1 tablespoon fresh mint
   leaves, chopped
Sea salt and freshly ground
   black pepper
900 ml (1¹/₂ pints) water
450 g (1 lb) lettuce leaves,
   washed and shredded
Crème fraîche to garnish

When the first lettuces of summer are ready the weather is often not quite warm enough for chilled soups. This warm lettuce soup also uses the early mint leaves usually growing at the same time. It can be made from the outer leaves of Cos, Webb's or other similar lettuce.

Melt the butter in a large pan and cook the onion until soft. Add the potatoes and half the mint leaves and mix well in the hot butter.

Season well and add the water. Bring to the boil and simmer for 10 minutes or until the potatoes are soft. Mash them with a fork and then stir in the shredded lettuce and the remaining mint leaves. Simmer for 2 minutes, taste and adjust seasoning. Serve at once. Top each bowl with a generous spoonful of crème fraîche.

CHESTNUT AND BACON SOUP

SERVES
—— 4 ——

As peeling fresh chestnuts is one of the more arduous culinary tasks, I have used tinned purée in this recipe. Do make sure the one you buy is unsweetened. This is a delicious winter soup with a distinctly Christmassy flavour.

Heat the oil in a large saucepan and fry the onion and bacon until lightly coloured. Add the garlic and cook for a further minute.

Beat the chestnut purée with a little stock or water to thin it and then add it to the pan along with the remaining stock or water, bay leaf, salt, pepper and nutmeg. Simmer for 15 minutes.

Taste the soup, add Tabasco and lemon juice, and adjust the seasoning.

Serve very hot with garlic croûtons.

INGREDIENTS

PREPARATION TIME
10 minutes
COOKING TIME
20 minutes

2 tablespoons olive oil
1 large onion, finely chopped
175 g (6 oz) smoked streaky bacon
1 garlic clove, crushed
1 × 450 g (1 lb) tin chesnut purée
900 ml (1½ pints) stock or water
1 bay leaf
Sea salt and freshly ground black pepper
About ¼ teaspoon freshly grated nutmeg
A few drops of Tabasco
Juice of 1 small lemon
Crisp garlic croûtons to serve (see p. 127)

RED BEET SOUP

SERVES

—— 4 ——

Beetroot has a wonderful colour and light sweet flavour that needs a little zing added. To do this I have used a dash of Tabasco and some fresh orange juice. Always use gloves when peeling beetroot.

PREPARATION TIME
15 minutes
COOKING TIME
20 minutes

4 medium beetroot, peeled
1 large onion
2 sticks celery
40 g (1¹/₂ oz) butter
Grated zest and juice of
  2 oranges
900 ml (1¹/₂ pints) vegetable
  or chicken stock
Sea salt and freshly ground
  black pepper
A few drops of Tabasco
Soured cream to garnish
Chopped fresh dill to garnish

Cut the beets, onion, and celery into chunks and place in the bowl of a food processor. Process until finely chopped.

Melt the butter in a large saucepan and cook the vegetables in it over a moderate heat for 3–4 minutes.

Add the orange zest and juice and the stock. Season lightly with salt, pepper and Tabasco and simmer for 15 minutes.

Taste and adjust the seasoning and serve hot with a blob of soured cream and a few fronds of chopped dill garnishing each bowl.

LENTIL AND VEGETABLE CHOWDER

SERVES

— 4 —

I first made this chowder with lentils having forgotten to buy some chicken pieces from the supermarket. I now make it often as it uses ingredients I keep in the fridge, is packed with good things, and feeds any vegetarians who happen to be eating with us.

Heat the oil in a large saucepan and fry the onion until soft. Add the garlic and vegetables and cook for 2 minutes.

Now add the remaining ingredients, seasoning lightly with pepper and salt. Bring to the boil and simmer for 20–30 minutes. Taste and adjust seasoning. Serve hot.

INGREDIENTS

PREPARATION TIME
10 minutes
COOKING TIME
25–35 minutes

1 tablespoon olive oil
1 large onion, chopped
1 plump garlic clove, crushed
2 medium leeks, washed and
    finely sliced
2 medium carrots, peeled and
    finely sliced
2 sticks celery, finely sliced
100 g (4 oz) baby corn,
    finely sliced
100 g (4 oz) open-cap
    mushrooms, sliced
2–3 sprigs fresh thyme
1.2 litres (2 pints) water
75 g (3 oz) red lentils
1 tablespoon tomato purée
Sea salt and freshly ground
    black pepper

TOMATO AND BREAD SOUP
WITH CHILLI OIL

S E R V E S
—— 4 ——

PREPARATION TIME
10 minutes
COOKING TIME
15 minutes

2 tablespoons olive oil
1 medium onion, chopped
1–2 plump garlic cloves,
   crushed
2 × 400 g (14 oz) tins
   chopped Italian tomatoes
1 teaspoon fresh thyme,
   tarragon or chervil leaves
600 ml (1 pint) water
Sea salt and freshly ground
   black pepper
About 4–6 slices country-
   style white bread
Chilli oil to taste
Chopped fresh parsley
   to garnish

Another simple Italian soup, this time thickened with bread. In summer this soup can be made with fresh tomatoes but, as few things are more unappetizing than tomato skin, you will have to allow a little extra time to peel your tomatoes. It may also be necessary to add a few extra tomatoes to give a good flavour. Just taste the soup as you go along.

Heat the oil in a large, heavy pan and fry the onion and garlic until soft and transparent.

Now add the tomatoes and mix well. Stir in the herbs, add the water and season well. Simmer for 5–10 minutes. Break up the slices of bread and add to the soup. Add only enough bread to give the texture you want, be it thick or thin.

Taste and adjust the seasoning and spoon into warmed bowls. Float a little chilli oil on the surface of each bowl and scatter over some chopped parsley.

PUMPKIN AND APPLE SOUP

SERVES

— 6 —

This delicious, golden, autumn soup can be served in a whole pumpkin 'tureen'.

Heat the oil in a large pan and fry the onion until golden. Add the vegetables and apples and cook for a further 2 minutes. Now add the water, sugar, ground coriander and season lightly with salt, pepper and Tabasco to taste. Bring to the boil and simmer for 15–20 minutes or until the vegetables are soft.

You can liquidize this soup or, for a more interesting texture, mash it roughly with a potato masher.

Serve hot with garlic bread.

PREPARATION TIME
15 minutes
COOKING TIME
25 minutes

3 tablespoons olive oil
1 large onion, finely chopped
2 garlic cloves, crushed
900 g (2 lb) pumpkin, de-
    seeded, peeled and cubed
2 large potatoes, peeled
    and diced
3 medium eating apples,
    peeled and sliced
1.2 litres (2 pints) water
1 teaspoon soft brown sugar
2 teaspoons ground coriander
Sea salt and freshly ground
    black pepper
A few drops of Tabasco
Garlic bread to serve
    (see p. 129)

BRUSSELS SPROUT SOUP

SERVES

—— 4 ——

PREPARATION TIME
10 minutes
COOKING TIME
20 minutes

2 tablespoons butter
1 large onion, finely chopped
2 medium potatoes, peeled
   and diced
Sea salt and freshly ground
   black pepper
Freshly ground nutmeg
900 ml (1¹/₂ pints) water
450 g (1 lb) very fresh
   Brussels sprouts
Single cream to garnish

The secret of this fresh-tasting soup is not to overcook the sprouts.

Melt the butter and fry the onion until soft. Add the potatoes, some salt, pepper and nutmeg and the water. Simmer until the potatoes are soft (about 10 minutes). Liquidize in small batches.

In the food processor finely grate the sprouts. Return the soup to the pan and add the sprouts. Simmer for 3–4 minutes. Taste and adjust the seasoning.

Serve hot topped with a swirl of cream.

CORN SOUP WITH HERB-SPIKED CRÈME FRAÎCHE

SERVES

—— 4 ——

Fresh corn has wonderfully sweet, milky kernels – perfect for a delicate summer soup.

Melt the butter in a large pan and cook the onion until soft. Add the corn kernels and toss well.

Now put in the remaining soup ingredients, seasoning lightly. Simmer for 10 minutes while you make the Herb-spiked crème fraîche by simply mixing all the ingredients together. Allow to stand for 5 minutes.

Remove the corn cobs from the soup and discard and liquidize it. Rub through a sieve, taste and adjust seasoning, and serve hot topped with some of the crème fraîche.

INGREDIENTS

PREPARATION TIME
10 minutes + 2–3 minutes
sieving
COOKING TIME
15 minutes

---

50 g (2 oz) butter
1 large onion, chopped
Kernels cut from 4 cobs of
  fresh corn
4 sprigs fresh thyme
Sea salt and freshly ground
  black pepper
900 ml (1¹/₂ pints) water
2 corn cobs, cut into 5 cm
  (2 inch) pieces
1 quantity of herb-spiked
  crème fraîche (see p. 128)

CARROT, ORANGE AND CARDAMOM SOUP

SERVES
—— 4 ——

Carrots and oranges have a wonderful affinity which, in this soup, is enhanced by the addition of fragrant cardamom. This soup can be served topped with a little cream and some fresh chopped parsley.

Heat the oil in a large pan and fry the onion and carrot for 2–3 minutes. Add the cardamom seeds and cinnamon stick, then the orange juice, seasoning and water.

Simmer until the carrots are soft then liquidize. Taste the soup and season. Serve hot.

INGREDIENTS

PREPARATION TIME
10 minutes
COOKING TIME
15 minutes

2 tablespoons oil
1 large onion, finely chopped
450 g (1 lb) carrots, peeled and chopped
Seeds from 4 cardamom pods, crushed
1 × 4 inch cinnamon stick
600 ml (1 pint) orange juice
Sea salt and freshly ground black pepper
600 ml (1 pint) water

WATERCRESS SOUP

S E R V E S

—— 4–6 ——

A lovely summer or winter soup watercress has a peppery bite that tastes good hot or cold. Spinach soup can also be made using this recipe and, amid howls of protest from my publisher, I would suggest that the topmost leaves of weeds such as nettles, sorrel and wild garlic could also be substituted for watercress.

Melt the butter in a large pan and cook the onion until soft. Do not let it brown. Add half the watercress, the potatoes, water and some seasoning and simmer until the potatoes are soft (about 10–15 minutes).

Liquidize in batches, adding the remaining watercress to the last batch. This gives the soup a bright colour and clean fresh taste. Re-heat to boiling point and serve.

To make weed or spinach soup cook the potato/onion mixture for 5 minutes before adding all the chopped leaves. Simmer for a further 4–5 minutes before liquidizing.

INGREDIENTS

PREPARATION TIME
10 minutes
COOKING TIME
15–20 minutes

2 tablespoons butter
1 onion, chopped
2 bunches of fresh dark green
  watercress, roughly chopped
2 large potatoes, peeled
  and cubed
900 ml (1¹/₂ pints) water
Sea salt and freshly ground
  black pepper

JERUSALEM ARTICHOKE, ORANGE AND FRESH CORIANDER SOUP

SERVES
—— 4 ——

PREPARATION TIME
10 minutes
COOKING TIME
10 minutes

25 g (1 oz) butter
1 large onion, sliced
450 g (1 lb) large Jerusalem
  artichokes
Grated zest and juice of
  2 oranges
Sea salt and freshly ground
  black pepper
150 ml (5 fl oz) single cream
Small bunch fresh coriander
600 ml (1 pint) stock or
  water
Crisp garlic croûtons to serve
  (see p. 127)

While artichokes do take a little time to prepare, when I tested this recipe the soup took only 20 minutes to make including the time it took to peel the tubers.

Melt the butter in a large saucepan and add the onion. Cook over a low heat while you peel the artichokes. (I use a potato peeler.) As they are ready cut them into chunks and put into the pan. The smaller you cut the pieces the quicker they will cook.

Next add the orange juice and zest, a little salt and some pepper and bring to the boil. Cover with a close-fitting lid and simmer for 5–8 minutes or until the vegetables are soft.

Tip the vegetables and the pan juices into a blender or liquidizer and whiz until smooth. Reserve some coriander leaves and now add the cream and coriander and whiz until the herbs are finely chopped.

Return the thick purée to a clean saucepan and dilute to taste with stock or water. Adjust the seasoning and serve garnished with the reserved whole coriander leaves and some crunchy croûtons.

COURGETTE AND CARROT SOUP

S E R V E S

—— 4 ——

A very quick, fresh, summery soup. To peel the toma-toes, cover them in boiling water for 2 minutes, then drain and slip off the skins. A food processor grates the vegetables in seconds.

—————

Fry the shallots in the oil until soft, then toss the carrots, tomatoes and courgettes in the oil and add the stock. Simmer for 10 minutes. Taste and adjust the seasoning. For a smoother texture you could whiz the soup in the blender or liquidizer.

Serve hot.

INGREDIENTS

PREPARATION TIME
10 minutes
COOKING TIME
15 minutes

2 medium shallots, chopped
1 tablespoon oil
3 medium carrots, peeled
   and grated
225 g (8 oz) ripe tomatoes,
   peeled and chopped
3 medium courgettes, grated
900 ml (1¹/₂ pints) vegetable
   or chicken stock
Sea salt and freshly ground
   black pepper

STORE-CUPBOARD VEGETABLE SOUP

SERVES
—— 4 ——

PREPARATION TIME
10 minutes
COOKING TIME
15 minutes

2 tablespoons olive oil

1 onion, chopped

2 garlic cloves, chopped

1 × 400 g (14 oz) tin
chopped Italian tomatoes

1 × 400 g (14 oz) tin chick
peas or borlotti beans,
drained

1 × 400 g (14 oz) tin
artichoke hearts, drained
and quartered

$^1/_2$ teaspoon freeze-dried
mixed herbs

Sea salt and freshly ground
black pepper

A few drops of Tabasco

600 ml (1 pint) vegetable
stock

Green pesto sauce to serve

This is the soup to choose when the fridge looks bare and you gaze in dismay at the assortment of tins on the shelf. I would use a stock cube to add a little extra flavour and make substitutions as necessary for the vegetables. You could add frozen beans, broccoli or corn though I'm not sure about peas.

Heat the oil in a large saucepan and cook the onion until transparent. Add the garlic and cook for 1 minute. Tip in the tinned beans and vegetables. Add the herbs, a little seasoning and Tabasco and the stock. Bring to the boil and simmer for 10 minutes.

Serve in heated soup bowls topped with a spoonful of rich green pesto.

TOMATO AND TARRAGON SOUP

SERVES
—— 4–6 ——

When you see a glut of tomatoes, whether in the garden or at the shops, buy them and make this wonderful fresh tomato soup. It really does need 2 kg (4¹/₂ lb) to give the rich tomato flavour that knocks spots off the tinned version. If you wish you can add some garlic when cooking the shallots.

Chop the tomatoes roughly, making sure you keep all the juice. Heat the oil in a large pan and cook the shallots until soft.

Now put the tomatoes into the pan along with salt, pepper and most of the tarragon, reserving some leaves for later. Put a lid over the pan and cook on a very low heat for about 20 minutes.

Place the contents of the pan in a blender or liquidizer and process until smooth. Rub this purée through a sieve and then return to a clean pan. Bring to the boil and add about 600 ml (1 pint) of water or vegetable stock to thin the soup to your liking. Taste and adjust the seasoning then serve garnished with the reserved tarragon leaves.

INGREDIENTS

PREPARATION TIME
10 minutes
COOKING TIME
25 minutes

2 kg (4¹/₂ lb) ripe tomatoes
  plus calyxes
3 tablespoons good olive oil
2–3 shallots, chopped
Sea salt and freshly ground
  black pepper
A good handful of fresh
  tarragon leaves and stems

TUSCAN TOMATO AND BEAN SOUP

SERVES
4

PREPARATION TIME
10 minutes
COOKING TIME
15 minutes

1 medium onion, chopped
1–2 plump garlic cloves,
  crushed
2 tablespoons olive oil
1 × 400 g (14 oz) tin
  chopped Italian tomatoes
1 × 400 g (14 oz) tin
  cannellini beans, drained
900 ml (1¹/₂ pints) water or
  vegetable stock
Sea salt and freshly ground
  black pepper
Chopped fresh chervil or basil
Flaked fresh Parmesan to
  serve
Extra virgin olive oil to serve

Wonderful gutsy vegetable soups are found throughout Italy and this bean and tomato soup is one that I
particularly love. Use Italian tinned tomatoes plus a tin of
ready-cooked cannellini beans. Add a fresh blast of flavour
by using fresh herbs such as basil or chervil and finish with
extra virgin oil.

Ham stock adds a wonderful flavour to bean soup, so do
use this if you have some. It is easily made: put a ham bone,
seasoning vegetables such as onions, carrots and celery, and
bay leaves in a saucepan. Cover with water and simmer for
60 minutes.

In a large pan slowly sweat the onion and garlic in the olive
oil until transparent. Add the tomatoes, drained beans and
the stock. Season well and then simmer for 5–7 minutes.
Stir in the herbs, taste and adjust the seasoning, and serve
with flakes of fresh Parmesan, a drizzle of extra virgin olive
oil and plenty of fresh bread.

FISH SOUPS

Fish soups are in general very quick to make and so fit very appropriately into this book. Such a wide variety of fish available in supermarkets comes ready-skinned and boned that most of the work is done for you. Frozen fish fillets, prawns and even bags of mixed seafood all make good standbys. Cube the fish while still frozen and allow a few extra seconds' cooking time. Either use a fresh fish stock (see p. 20), dashi (a Japanese soup base made from dried tuna and available in sachet form, which keeps well, from health food shops and oriental supermarkets) or water to make your fish soups and never boil the soup rapidly once the fish has been added because fish toughens rapidly and becomes horribly stringy.

CONTENTS

New york-style haddock chowder

S E R V E S

—— 4 ——

There are two types of chowder commonly found in America: white potato-based soups mainly from New England, and spicy tomato ones from their racier cousins in New York. I've used haddock here but you could use clams or any other white fish.

Melt the butter in a large pan and fry the onion until soft. Add all the remaining vegetables except for the tomatoes and stir and fry for a further 2–3 minutes. Now pour in the tomatoes and half of the water and some seasoning and simmer for 10 minutes.

Mash the potatoes a little with the back of a spoon. Now add the cubed fish and continue to cook for a further 2–3 minutes. Taste and adjust the seasoning, adding more water if needed.

Serve hot.

INGREDIENTS

PREPARATION TIME
10 minutes
COOKING TIME
20 minutes

25 g (1 oz) butter
1 medium onion, finely
  chopped
1 medium carrot, peeled
  and chopped
1 stick celery, chopped
1 green pepper, de-seeded
  and chopped
1 large potato, peeled
  and diced
1 × 400 g (14 oz) tin
  chopped Italian tomatoes
600 ml (1 pint) water
Sea salt and freshly ground
  black pepper
350 g (12 oz) haddock
  (skinned and boned
  weight), cut into cubes

CULLEN SKINK

SERVES

—— 4 ——

PREPARATION TIME
10 minutes
COOKING TIME
20 minutes

25 g (1 oz) butter
1 medium onion, finely
  chopped
1 medium leek, cleaned
  and chopped
3 medium potatoes, peeled
  and diced
600 ml (1 pint) water
225 g (8 oz) smoked
  haddock (skinned and
  boned weight), cut
  into cubes
300 ml (10 fl oz) milk
Sea salt and freshly ground
  black pepper
Chopped fresh parsley
  to garnish

This wonderful, tasty soup mixes potatoes with smoked haddock. Do try to buy undyed haddock or at least fish that has not been painted too luminous a yellow.

Skink is an old Scottish word for broth – this one is said to originate from the small fishing port of Cullen in northern Scotland.

Melt the butter in a pan and cook the onion, leek and potatoes for 2–3 minutes. Add the water and bring to the boil. Simmer for 7–10 minutes then mash the vegetables lightly with a spoon.

Add the cubed fish and the milk and simmer for 3–4 minutes. Taste and adjust the seasoning, adding pepper to taste and salt if needed.

Serve hot sprinkling with chopped parsley.

Opposite: RED BEET SOUP *(Page 50)*
CREAM OF ONION SOUP *(Page 37)*
AND CRISP GARLIC CROÛTONS *(Page 127)*

Overleaf: HADDOCK, PRAWN AND SWEETCORN CHOWDER *(Page 71)*.
CREAM OF MUSSEL SOUP *(Page 72)*

HADDOCK, PRAWN AND SWEETCORN CHOWDER

S E R V E S
—— 4 ——

This is a widely unauthentic chowder, but one that tastes delicious and looks wonderful. For extra speed, use frozen haddock fillets and 175 g (6 oz) of tinned chopped tomatoes.

Heat the oil in a large saucepan and fry the leeks and potatoes for 2–3 minutes. Do not allow them to brown.

Add the water, a little salt and pepper and bring to the boil. Simmer for 10 minutes or until the potatoes are nearly cooked. Mash roughly with a fork or potato masher.

Add the corn, haddock and tomatoes and simmer for 3 4 minutes

Taste and adjust the seasoning. Add the prawns, heat through and serve the soup garnished with the coriander.

INGREDIENTS

PREPARATION TIME
15 minutes
COOKING TIME
20 minutes

2 tablespoons oil
2 leeks, washed and sliced
3 medium potatoes, peeled and diced
900 ml (1¹/₂ pints) water
Sea salt and freshly ground black pepper
175 g (6 oz) tinned sweetcorn kernels
225 g (8 oz) fresh haddock (skinned and boned weight), cut into cubes
2–3 medium tomatoes, skinned and chopped
100 g (4 oz) cooked, peeled prawns
Chopped fresh coriander to garnish

Preceding page: YELLOW PEPPER SOUP *(Page 45)*
BRUSSELS SPROUT SOUP *(Page 54)*

Opposite: CHILLI BEEF SOUP *(Page 93)*
CHICKEN PEPPERPOT SOUP *(Page 89)*

CREAM OF MUSSEL SOUP

S E R V E S

—— 4 ——

PREPARATION TIME
10 minutes
COOKING TIME
10 minutes

25 g (1 oz) butter
2 shallots, chopped
1 heaped tablespoon plain
flour
600 ml (1 pint) skimmed
milk
300 ml (10 fl oz) water
Sea salt and freshly ground
black pepper
2 tablespoons dry sherry
1 tablespoon Thai fish sauce
(nam prik)
50 g (2 oz) button
mushrooms, finely sliced
225 g (8 oz) ready-cooked
mussels or equivalent
(see above)
2 tablespoons chopped fresh
chervil or tarragon
to garnish

If time doesn't permit steaming your own use pre-cooked mussels, available from supermarkets, or well-drained jars of mussels for this soup. Should you be able to buy ready-cleaned mussels cook them in a large pan with 2–3 table-spoons water or wine until all the shells have opened, discarding any that stay resolutely closed and add to the soup, complete with the strained cooking liquor.

Fresh oysters are held to be too costly to put into soup even though their delicate flavour is to me even more delicious when the molluscs have been warmed through. I have sometimes used a tin of smoked oysters for this soup – much easier to prise open!

Melt the butter in a large pan and fry the shallots until soft. Now add the flour and mix well. Blend in the milk and water and season with a little salt and pepper.

Simmer the sauce for 2–3 minutes until the flour is cooked. Now add the sherry, the Thai fish sauce and the mushrooms. Cook for a further 2 minutes.

Carefully stir in the chosen molluscs and warm through. Serve at once scattered with the fresh herbs.

CRAB AND SWEETCORN SOUP

SERVES

—— 4 ——

A favourite soup from Chinese restaurants, chopped cooked chicken can be substituted for crab in this recipe.

Place the well drained crab meat in a bowl and pour on the soy sauce.

Bring the stock to the boil in a large saucepan. If you use a stock cube for this recipe dilute with an extra 300 ml ('/₂ pint) of water and reserve 300 ml ('/₂ pint) of stock for another use.

Add the corn to the stock and bring back to the boil. Mix the cornflour and water and stir thoroughly into the soup. Simmer for 2 minutes or until no raw taste remains. Now add the crab and bring back to boiling point.

Beat the egg white a little to break it down then stir this into the gently simmering soup. Cook for a further 30 seconds.

Serve at once garnished with finely chopped spring onions and prawn crackers.

INGREDIENTS

PREPARATION TIME
10 minutes
COOKING TIME
10 minutes

175 g (6 oz) tin crab meat in brine, well drained
1 tablespoon soy sauce
1 pint chicken or other light stock
425g (15 oz) tin creamed style sweetcorn
1 tablespoon cornflour
2 tablespoons water
1 egg white

TO SERVE
Spring onions and prawn crackers.

BOURRIDE OF FISH

SERVES

—— 4 ——

PREPARATION TIME
**10 minutes + 5 minutes for
the mayonnaise**
COOKING TIME
10 minutes

*450 g (1 lb) prepared fish
(see above)*
900 ml (1¹/₂ pints) water
1 fish or vegetable stock cube
*1 leek, cleaned and
finely sliced*
*2 carrots, peeled and
finely sliced*
2 sticks celery, finely sliced

FOR THE MAYONNAISE
1 egg yolk
1 dessertspoon wine vinegar
1 plump garlic clove
*Sea salt and freshly ground
black pepper*
120 ml (4 fl oz) olive oil
*Chopped fresh chives
to garnish*

Using mayonnaise to thicken and enrich soups is an idea from France. You must not boil the soup once the mayonnaise has been added and you must use home-made mayonnaise because it does not contain emulsifiers or stabilizers. Apart from that the recipe is very simple. I sometimes use a tray of mixed cooked shellfish, molluscs and squid, as sold in supermarkets. Alternatively you can use some scallops mixed with skinned and boned fillets of cod and salmon.

If using fresh fish cut it into 2.5 cm (1 inch) cubes, slicing scallops in half. Put the water, crumbled stock cube and the prepared vegetables into a large saucepan and bring to the boil. Cover and simmer for 5 minutes.

Meanwhile make the mayonnaise: in a food processor whiz the egg yolk, vinegar, garlic and a little seasoning together. With the motor running add the oil in a very fine stream, continuing until the mayonnaise thickens and all the oil is used.

Now add the fish to the pan. If you are using raw fish bring to the boil and gentle simmer for about 2 minutes. If the fish and shellfish is already cooked just heat it through gently.

Pour a small ladleful of hot stock into the mayonnaise and mix. Remove the pan from the heat. Add the mayonnaise mixture to the soup, stirring carefully so as not to break up the fish and serve at once in warm bowls scattered with the fresh chives.

SPINACH AND PRAWN SOUP

S E R V E S

—— 4 ——

This is a very pretty summer dish. Warm the prawns through at the last moment, then float them on the creamy green soup.

Melt the butter in a large pan and fry the shallots until soft. Add the potatoes and cook for a further minute. Now pour in the water, season lightly and simmer for 10 minutes. Add the shredded spinach and simmer for a further 2 minutes.

Liquidize the soup in small batches and pour into a clean pan. Add a squeeze of lemon juice and stir in the cream. Then re-heat the soup. Taste and adjust the seasoning.

Keep the soup warm while you heat the prawns but do not allow it to boil.

In a pan melt the knob of butter, add the chilli powder and black pepper. Sauté the prawns for 2 minutes or until hot, then spoon onto the soup. Serve at once.

INGREDIENTS

PREPARATION TIME
10 minutes
COOKING TIME
15 minutes + 2 minutes for prawns

25 g (1 oz) butter
2 shallots, finely chopped
2 medium potatoes, peeled and diced
600 ml (1 pint) water
Sea salt and freshly ground black pepper
450 g (1 lb) bag of spinach, washed and shredded
A squeeze of lemon juice
150 ml (5 fl oz) single cream
A knob of butter
A pinch of chilli powder
A pinch of freshly ground black pepper
175 g (6 oz) cooked, peeled prawns

PRAWN GUMBO

S E R V E S

—— 6 ——

PREPARATION TIME
15 minutes
COOKING TIME
35 minutes

120 ml (4 fl oz) vegetable oil
1 large oinion
3 sticks celery
1 small green pepper,
 de-seeded
2-3 garlic cloves
100 g (4 oz) plain flour
100 g (4 oz) smoked ham or
 sausage, chopped
450 g (1 lb) skinned and
 boned white fish (cod,
 haddock or monkfish), cut
 into cubes
1.5 litres (2¹/₂ pints) fish or
 chicken stock
1 × 225 g (8 oz) tin white
 crabmeat (optional)
1 bunch spring onions,
 chopped
Sea salt and freshly ground
 black pepper
A few drops of Tabasco
225 g (8 oz) cooked
 peeled prawns
2 tablespoons chopped
 fresh parsley

Gumbo comes from the American deep south – a traditional dish of the Creole/Cajun triangle that lies
between New Orleans, Lafayette and Baton Rouge. The
regional cooking there is based on two staples: the roux,
flour and fat slowly browned; and the trinity, a mixture of
chopped celery, pepper and onion.

This is a luxury dish filled with good things that would
make the centrepiece of a meal. Put a pan of long-grain rice
on to cook at the same time as the soup simmers and serve a
spoonful in each bowl. Don't be put off by the length of
the recipe the soup is very simple to make.

———

Heat the oil in a large heavy pan until very hot. Meanwhile
chop the vegetables in a food processor until fine. When
the oil is ready add the flour and, stirring constantly, cook
until this roux is pale golden.

Now add the vegetables. They will start to sizzle at once,
cooling the roux and stopping it from burning. Add the
chopped ham or sausage and half the prepared fish. A little
at a time add the stock, stirring constantly.

Simmer for 20 minutes. Add all the remaining ingredients except the prawns and parsley, and simmer for a further
5 minutes. Stir in the prawns and parsley, heat through,
adjust the seasonings and serve with boiled rice.

SMOKED HADDOCK AND TOMATO BROTH WITH CHEESE CROÛTONS

S E R V E S
—— 4 ——

Try to find undyed fish for this recipe. You can use smoked cod instead of haddock if you wish.

Remove the skin and bones from the fish and cut the flesh into small pieces. Heat the stock with the leeks in a large pan and simmer for 5 minutes.

Add the tomatoes, fish and herbs and continue to cook for 2–3 minutes or until the fish is opaque.

Mix the cream with the egg yolk and, having heated the soup to boiling point, remove it from the stove and mix in the cream. The soup should thicken very slightly.

Taste and adjust the seasoning and serve at once garnished with the hot cheese croûtons.

INGREDIENTS

PREPARATION TIME
10 minutes
COOKING TIME
10 minutes

350 g (12 oz) smoked haddock
900 ml (1¹/₂ pints) fish stock
2 medium leeks, cleaned and finely sliced
3 fresh plum tomatoes, peeled and diced
1 tablespoon chopped fresh chives
1 tablespoon chopped fresh parsley
4 tablespoons single cream
1 egg yolk
Sea salt and freshly ground black pepper
Cheese croûtons to serve (see p. 127)

CREAM OF SALMON SOUP

S E R V E S
—— 4 ——

PREPARATION TIME
10 minutes
COOKING TIME
20 minutes

*275 g (10 oz) fresh salmon
(skinned, boned weight)*
1 tablespoon light oil
1 tablespoon butter
2 shallots, chopped
1 stick celery, finely diced
*1 heaped tablespoon plain
flour*
120 ml (4 fl oz) white wine
*300 ml (10 fl oz) fish stock
or water*
*Sea salt and freshly ground
black pepper*
1 bay leaf
*2 tablespoons chopped fresh
dill or tarragon*
300 ml (10 fl oz) milk
A few drops of lemon juice
A few drops of Tabasco
*Fresh dill or tarragon
to garnish*

This luxurious, elegant soup would be a delightful way to start a dinner party. Use whatever white wine you will be drinking with the meal and remember the soup must not be boiled after the milk has been added.

Cut the fish into 2.5 cm (1 inch) cubes. Reserve about 6 of these, cutting them into tiny dice.

Heat the oil and butter in a large pan and cook the shallots and celery until transparent. Add the flour and stir well. Now add the wine and stock and bring to the boil, stirring constantly, to give a smooth soup.

Season lightly, add the bay leaf and simmer for 5 minutes. Now add the fish and chopped herbs and cook for a further 2–3 minutes. Remove the bay leaf. Liquidize the mixture and return to a clean pan.

Dilute the soup with the milk and adjust the seasoning, adding a few drops of lemon juice and Tabasco to balance the flavours. Bring up to a simmer and add the tiny dice of salmon. Keep just at simmering point for a minute, then serve garnished with a few fronds of fresh dill or tarragon.

COD AND POTATO SOUP WITH PESTO

S E R V E S
—— 4 ——

Use any white fish for this recipe. If you want to use frozen fillets, cut the fish into cubes to speed thawing time before adding to the soup.

———

Heat the oil in a large pan and fry the onion until soft. Add the garlic, potatoes and leek, turning them a few times in the oil. Then add the water or stock, season lightly and bring to the boil. Cook for 10 minutes then mash with a fork gently to break up the potatoes a little.

Cut the cod into 2.5 cm (1 inch) cubes and add to the soup, simmer for 3–4 minutes then taste and adjust the seasoning. Stir in the spring onions.

Serve in warm soup bowls topping each portion with a spoonful of pesto sauce.

INGREDIENTS

PREPARATION TIME
10 minutes
COOKING TIME
20 minutes

2 tablespoons olive oil
1 onion, chopped
1 plump garlic clove, crushed
3 medium potatoes, peeled
 and diced
1 medium leek, cleaned and
 finely sliced
900 ml (1¹/₂ pints) fish stock
 or water
Sea salt and freshly ground
 black pepper
350 g (12 oz) fresh cod or
 haddock (skinned and
 boned weight)
2 spring onions, chopped
4-5 tablespoons pesto sauce
 to serve

SUMMER VEGETABLE AND FISH SOUP

SERVES
—— 4 ——

This is a lovely brothy, soup fragrant with the flavours of summer. Serve the soup topped with slices of French bread and Parmesan.

Heat the oil in a large pan and cook the onion until it softens. Add the pepper and garlic and cook for a further 2–3 minutes. Now add the tomatoes, thyme, some seasoning and the stock or water and simmer for 5 minutes.

Put the pasta into the broth and cook for 2 minutes. Cut the fish into 1 cm ($\frac{1}{2}$ inch) cubes and add to the soup along with the courgettes. Simmer for 2 minutes.

Adjust the seasoning and stir in the torn basil leaves. Serve at once topping each dish with a piece of French bread and some Parmesan.

INGREDIENTS

PREPARATION TIME
15 minutes
COOKING TIME
15 minutes

2 tablespoons olive oil
1 large onion, chopped
1 red pepper, de-seeded and
  finely sliced
1-2 plump garlic cloves,
  crushed
1 × 200 g (7 oz) tin chopped
  Italian tomatoes
2-3 sprigs fresh thyme
Sea salt and freshly ground
  black pepper
900 ml (1½ pints) fish stock
  or water
100 g (4 oz) fresh tagliatelle
350 g (12 oz) firm white fish
  (skinned and boned
  weight)
2 medium courgettes,
  finely sliced
3-4 sprigs fresh basil,
  roughly torn

TO SERVE
A few thin slices French
  bread, toasted
Freshly grated Parmesan

MEDITERRANEAN FISH SOUP WITH ROUILLE

SERVES
— 4 —

Popular all the way along the south coast of France, this soup in fact comes from the region around Marseilles. It will have a much fuller flavour if you use fish stock.

Put the oil into a large pan and cook the onion, garlic and vegetables until soft. Add the tomatoes, wine, herbs and seasoning and simmer for 20 minutes.

While the soup is simmering, make the rouille by placing everything but the oil in a blender and whizzing it until very smooth. Add the oil in a thin stream. Put the rouille in a bowl for serving.

Liquidize the soup in small batches.

Re-heat and add the prepared fish. Gently simmer for 2–3 minutes or until the fish is just opaque.

Serve hot with slices of toasted French bread, rouille (spread a little on a piece of the bread and float in the soup) and grated Gruyère.

INGREDIENTS

PREPARATION TIME
15 minutes
COOKING TIME
25 minutes

2 tablespoons olive oil
1 onion, finely chopped
2–3 plump garlic cloves, chopped
1 carrot, peeled and finely chopped
1 stick celery, finely chopped
2 × 400 g (14 oz) tins chopped tomatoes
¼ bottle white wine
½ teaspoon dried herbes de Provence
Sea salt and freshly ground black pepper
450 g (1 lb) mixed fish: monkfish, hake, salmon, prawns, cooked mussels etc. (prepared weight)
900 ml (1 ½ pints) fish stock or water

FOR THE ROUILLE
1 × 200 g (7 oz) tin red pimientos, drained
1 fresh red chilli seeded
2 plump cloves garlic
2 thick slices white bread
Salt and pepper
150 ml (5 fl oz) olive oil

TO SERVE
Slices of French bread, toasted
Grated Gruyère

New england clam chowder

S E R V E S
—— 4 ——

PREPARATION TIME
10 minutes
COOKING TIME
20 minutes

3 tablespoons butter
1 large onion, finely chopped
50 g (2 oz) piece bacon,
  rinded and diced
2 large potatoes, peeled
  and diced
600 ml (1 pint) milk
Freshly ground black pepper
1 × 200 g (7 oz) shelled
  clams
2 tablespoons chopped fresh
  parsley

Now for the other American-style chowder. Don't overboil the clams or they will become tough, resembling little rubber balls. If you can buy clams in their own juice don't throw the liquor away, but simply drain and add it to the soup along with the milk, adjusting the quantity accordingly.

Heat the butter in a large pan and add the onion and bacon. Cook for 4–5 minutes until both are soft.

Now add the potatoes and milk, seasoning with a little pepper. Bring to the boil and simmer for 10 minutes.

Drain the clams well and add to the soup. Simmer for 2–3 minutes then scatter on the chopped parsley and serve at once.

MEAT AND POULTRY SOUPS

When the weather is cold and wet I long for a bowl of soup. And few things are more calculated to cheer after a trudge home in the rain than a steaming chunky soup. The tantalizing smells that fill the kitchen are a promise of the good things to come and while, at first glance, meat soups might seem far from quick to make many of the soups in this chapter use instant ingredients like the *German Sausage Soup and Noodles* (p. 91) or the wonderfully rich and creamy *Chicken Pepperpot Soup* (p. 89).

Not all the soups are peasant style. *Chicken Waterzoi* (p. 96), a Belgian soup, is light and delicious and *White Soup* (p. 87) the very pinacle of elegance. For days when you fancy adding a little spice to life *Chilli beef* (p. 93), *Chicken Mulligatawny* (p. 98) and *Hungarian Goulash Soup* (p. 94) are all you would expect, rustic and robust.

These are real rib-sticking soups. Serve them with hot bread and a glass of red wine and you have a meal to dispel the most lingering of winter blues.

CONTENTS

PHEASANT AND CHESTNUT SOUP

S E R V E S

—— 6 ——

This recipe comes from my friend Shaun Hill, the delightful and talented Irish chef, and, while at first glance it may not look quick, it is very easy. Pheasant is widely available, during the game season, from supermarkets or from butchers.

———

Fry the onion and garlic in the butter until soft. Put the pheasant into the pan and brown on all sides. Add the spices, chestnut purée and tomatoes and fry for a few moments.

Pour in the water and season lightly. Simmer for 30 minutes. Remove the pheasant from the pot and cut off the breast meat. Reserve this.

Roughly remove the leg meat and return it to the soup. Liquidize this in batches and pour into a clean pan. Chop the breast meat and stir in.

Re-heat the soup, adjust the seasoning, adding lemon juice to taste, then serve garnished with a little cream in each bowl.

INGREDIENTS

PREPARATION TIME
15 minutes
COOKING TIME
40 minutes

1 medium onion, finely
   choppped
1 garlic clove, crushed
A knob of butter
1 hen pheasant
1 × 4 inch cinnamon stick
$^{1}/_{4}$ nutmeg, grated
225 g (8 oz) unsweetened
   chestnut purée
2 peeled tinned Italian
   tomatoes, chopped
1.2 litres (2 pints) water
Sea salt and freshly ground
   black pepper
Lemon juice to taste
1 tablespoon cream to garnish

CHICKEN, LENTIL AND APRICOT SOUP

SERVES
—— 6 ——

This chunky soup is again based on the happy combination of chicken and lentils. The addition of apricots and cinnamon give the soup a Turkish, sweet/sour flavour. Serve it with a spoonful of smatana or soured cream.

Heat the oil in a large saucepan and cook the onion, garlic, celery and carrot for 2–3 minutes.

Add the chicken meat and the apricots and stir well. Now put in the tinned tomatoes, lentils and water.

Season with pepper and cinnamon and bring to the boil. Simmer for 20 minutes then taste, adding salt and adjusting the seasoning.

Serve hot topped with spoonfuls of soured cream.

INGREDIENTS

PREPARATION TIME
10 minutes
COOKING TIME
30 minutes

2 tablespoons olive oil
1 large onion, chopped
1 garlic clove, crushed
2 sticks celery, sliced
2 carrots, peeled and sliced
2 boned, skinless chicken
   breasts or 6 boned, skinless
   thighs, diced
50 g (2 oz) ready-to-eat
   dried apricots
1 × 400 g (14 oz) tin
   chopped Italian tomatoes
100 g (4 oz) red lentils
1.2 litres (2 pints) water
Sea salt and freshly ground
   black pepper
1-2 teaspoons ground
   cinnamon to taste
Soured cream to serve

WHITE SOUP

S E R V E S

—— 4 ——

Popular since Tudor times and mentioned by Jane Austen in *Pride and Prejudice*, white soup is delicious and simple to make. You must use good chicken stock and fresh almonds. Don't forget that, if you use it, chill-fresh stock from supermarkets is usually sold double strength.

Process the almonds in a food processor until finely chopped. Add a little stock and process for a further 1-2 minutes.

Tip this mixture into a large saucepan, add the remaining stock and simmer for 15 minutes.

Season with salt and pepper to taste and serve hot garnished with the chives.

INGREDIENTS

PREPARATION TIME
5 minutes
COOKING TIME
15 minutes

100 g (4 oz) whole blanched almonds
1.2 litres (2 pints) chicken stock (either home-made or chill-fresh)
Sea salt and white pepper
1 tablespoon chopped fresh chives to garnish

HAM AND CHICK PEA CHOWDER

SERVES
—— 6 ——

PREPARATION TIME
10 minutes
COOKING TIME
30 minutes

2 tablespoons oil
1 large onion, finely chopped
2 garlic cloves, crushed
225 g (8 oz) ham or
    gammon steak, chopped
1 × 400 g (14 oz) tin chick
    peas, drained
600 ml (1 pint) passata
1 teaspoon freeze-dried mixed
    herbs
Sea salt and freshly ground
    black pepper
A few drops of Tabasco
600 ml (1 pint) water
    or stock

Another robust soup this time using a chunk of ham and some chick peas. If you have a piece of ham left over from a joint so much the better, if not use a couple of gammon steaks. Passata is sieved Italian tomatoes. It is a wonderfully fresh-tasting ingredient that gives all the flavour of tomato without any skin or pips!

Heat the oil in a large pan and fry the onion, garlic, and ham or gammon for 3–4 minutes. Add the chick peas, passata, herbs and some salt and pepper, Tabasco and half the stock or water. Bring to the boil.

Simmer for 15–20 minutes, adjust the seasoning and add more stock if necessary and serve.

CHICKEN PEPPERPOT SOUP

S E R V E S

—— 4 ——

Smooth as silk, this soup has a delicate creamy flavour spiked with red and green sweet peppers. Flour may be a very unfashionable ingredient but properly cooked it adds a stable velvet-like texture to cream soups.

Reserve a few slices of red and green pepper for garnish. Melt the butter in a large saucepan and cook the shallots until soft. Now add the peppers and continue to cook until they too soften.

Put in the chicken. Turn this well in the hot fat to seal the meat but do not let it colour.

Sprinkle over the flour and stir well to make sure it is all absorbed by the butter. Now slowly add the milk, stirring constantly. Bring the soup to a simmer and leave to cook for 10 minutes. Add the water or stock and season to taste.

Serve hot scattered with the chopped, reserved red and green pepper.

INGREDIENTS

PREPARATION TIME
10 minutes
COOKING TIME
20 minutes

50 g (2 oz) butter
2 shallots, finely chopped
1 small red pepper, de-seeded and finely sliced
1 small green pepper, de-seeded and finely sliced
2 boned, skinless chicken breasts, finely chopped
25 g (1 oz) plain flour
600 ml (1 pint) semi-skimmed milk
300 ml (10 fl oz) water or stock
Sea Salt and freshly ground black pepper

BEEF SOUP WITH HERB DUMPLINGS

SERVES

—— 4 ——

If you want to use a cheaper cut of meat that's fine, you will just need to cook the soup a little longer.

INGREDIENTS

PREPARATION TIME
15 minutes
COOKING TIME
20–45 minutes

100 g (4 oz) open-cap mushrooms, chopped
2 tablespoons beef dripping or butter
2 onions, chopped
1 carrot, peeled and diced
2 sticks celery, diced
225 g (8 oz) rump steak (trimmed weight)
1 tablespoon plain flour
1 × 200 g (7 oz) tin Italian tomatoes
1-2 sprigs fresh thyme
1 tablespoon Worcestershire sauce
1 tablespoon tomato purée
1¹/₂ pints (900 ml) stock or water
Sea salt and freshly ground black pepper

FOR THE DUMPLINGS
1 teaspoon baking powder
100 g (4 oz) plain flour
40 g (1¹/₂ oz) butter of block margarine
2 teaspoons chopped fresh herbs
3 tablespoons milk

Melt the dripping or butter in a pressure cooker or large, heavy pan. Add the onions, carrot and celery and cook, stirring often, until the vegetables soften. Turn up the heat and continue to fry until they start to brown.

Meanwhile trim any remaining fat and gristle from the steak and cut it into 1 cm ('/2 inch) cubes. Add these to the pan and, stirring constantly, cook until these too are browned. The bottom of the pan will be quite well coloured but don't worry, since this will add more flavour to the soup.

Sprinkle over the flour and stir to mix in. Add the mushrooms to the pan with the tomatoes. Stir well, then add the thyme, Worcestershire sauce, tomato purée and half the stock or water. Season. Bring up to pressure and cook for 15 minutes if using a pressure cooker or simmer for 40 minutes.

Meanwhile make the dumplings. Mix the baking powder into the flour and rub in the butter or margarine. This can be done in a food processor for more speed. Add the herbs, season well and mix to a firm dough with the milk.

Taste the soup and add extra salt and pepper if needed. Add enough extra stock to dilute to the desired consistency. Place spoonfuls of the dumpling mixture into the pot, pressing each just below the surface. Simmer for 4–5 minutes then serve in warmed soup bowls.

GERMAN SAUSAGE SOUP WITH NOODLES

S E R V E S

—— 4 ——

For this soup you will need to use the German-style sausages like bratwurst, good quality frankfurters or a Dutch boiling ring.

———

Heat the oil or lard in a large pan and fry the onion, garlic and vegetables for 2–3 minutes. Add the stock, herbs, salt and pepper and simmer for 10 minutes.

Now add the noodles and sausage pieces and continue to cook until the pasta is *al dente*. Taste and adjust the seasoning, the soup should be quite peppery.

Spoon into hot bowls and serve.

INGREDIENTS

PREPARATION TIME
10 minutes
COOKING TIME
25 minutes

Scant tablespoon vegetable oil or lard
1 large onion, chopped
1 garlic clove, crushed
2 carrots, peeled and sliced
2 leeks, cleaned and sliced
1.2 litres (2 pints) chicken or beef stock
A good pinch mixed dried herbs
Sea salt and freshly ground black pepper
225 g (8 oz) thick flat egg pasta noodles
350 g (12 oz) German-style sausages, cut into 2.5 cm (1 inch) chunks

SPLIT PEA AND HAM SOUP

S E R V E S

—— 4 ——

INGREDIENTS

PREPARATION TIME
10 minutes
COOKING TIME
50 minutes

175 g (6 oz) yellow split
  peas, washed
1.2 litres (2 pints) water
1 bay leaf
1 teaspoon fresh thyme leaves
2 medium leeks
1 plump garlic clove
100 g (4 oz) smoked ham
1 tablespoon olive oil
Sea salt and freshly ground
  black pepper

Split peas take about 45 minutes to cook (depending on their vintage) so while they simmer you can do any one of a number of things, only returning to the kitchen about 5 minutes before you want to eat in order to finish the soup.

Place the split peas and the water in a deep saucepan along with the herbs and bring to the boil. Simmer for 30–45 minutes or until soft.

Clean and slice the leeks, crush the garlic and chop the ham. Heat the oil in a frying-pan and cook the leeks and garlic until soft. Stir these plus the ham into the soup and season well. Simmer for a further 5 minutes. Serve hot.

CHILLI BEEF SOUP

SERVES

—— 6 ——

A perfect winter soup, this Tex Mex recipe comes from America. Add extra cayenne if you want a mouth-searing experience.

———————

In a large pan dry-fry the beef until the fat runs and the meat is well browned. Add the chopped onion, garlic and the oil and fry until coloured, adding more oil if necessary.

Now add the spices and oregano and stir and fry for a further minute.

Put the tinned tomatoes, beans and tomato purée into a blender or food processor and whiz for a few minutes to chop roughly. Add to the pan along with the salt and pepper and the water, bring to the boil and simmer for 15–20 minutes.

Check seasoning and adjust if necessary. Serve hot.

INGREDIENTS

PREPARATION TIME
10 minutes
COOKING TIME
30 minutes

225 g (8 oz) minced beef
2 plump garlic cloves, chopped
2 medium onions, finely chopped
1 tablespoon olive oil
2 teaspoons ground cumin
¹/₄ teaspoon cayenne pepper or to taste
3 teaspoons sweet paprika
1 teaspoon dried oregano
1 × 400 g (14 oz) tin chopped Italian tomatoes
1 × 400 g (14 oz) tin red kidney beans, drained
1 tablespoon tomato purée
¹/₂ teaspoon sea salt
Freshly ground black pepper
900 ml (1¹/₂ pints) water

HUNGARIAN GOULASH SOUP

SERVES

—— 6 ——

PREPARATION TIME
10 minutes
COOKING TIME
25-65 minutes

50 g (2 oz) lard
1 large onion, chopped
1 garlic clove, crushed
$^1/_2$ teaspoon caraway seeds
1 heaped tablespoon sweet
    paprika
$^1/_4$ teaspoon chilli powder
450 g (1 lb) steak, cut into
    small cubes
3 large potatoes, peeled
    and diced
1 red pepper, de-seeded
    and diced
1 × 400 g (14 oz) tin
    chopped Italian tomatoes
1.2 litres (2 pints) water
Salt and freshly ground black
    pepper

This Hungarian soup contains three types of pepper: powdered chilli, sweet paprika and fresh red pepper; plus another popular Eastern European seasoning, caraway seeds. It is quite definitely a meal-in-a-bowl. Once the ingredients have been assembled, it can be pressure-cooked for 20 minutes or can simmer away conventionally for 60 minutes.

Melt the lard in a pressure cooker or large saucepan and fry the onion until transparent. Add the garlic and caraway seeds and cook for a further 2–3 minutes.

Remove the pan from the heat and stir in the paprika and chilli powder. Add the meat and stir well. Return the pan to the heat and cook for a further minute. Add the remaining ingredients and bring to the boil.

If using a pressure cooker, bring up to pressure and cook for 20 minutes or, alternatively, simmer for 60 minutes, adding extra water if necessary. Taste and adjust the seasoning and serve.

TURKEY AND CRANBERRY SOUP

S E R V E S
—— 4 ——

This is really just a good way of using left-overs, so plentiful in those post-Christmas days, when penury leads to January and nothing looks more dreary than the well-picked turkey carcass.

INGREDIENTS

PREPARATION TIME
15 minutes
COOKING TIME
20 minutes

Heat the oil in a large pan and fry the vegetables and garlic for 2–3 minutes. Add the turkey meat, rice and tomatoes and stir well.

Mix in the cranberry relish, herbs, seasoning and stock, then bring to the boil and simmer for 15 minutes.

Taste and adjust the seasoning, adding extra water if necessary. Serve hot.

1 tablespoon olive oil
2 leeks, cleaned and sliced
2 carrots, peeled and sliced
2 sticks celery, sliced
1 garlic clove, chopped
225 g (8 oz) cooked turkey, diced
100 g (4 oz) basmati rice
6 sun-dried tomato halves, sliced
1 tablespoon cranberry relish
A good pinch of mixed dried herbs
Sea salt and freshly ground black pepper
1.2 litres (2 pints) chicken or vegetable stock

CHICKEN WATERZOI

SERVES

—— 4 ——

PREPARATION TIME
15 minutes
COOKING TIME
20 minutes

2 tablespoons butter
2 sticks celery, sliced
3 medium carrots, peeled and
    cut into julienne strips
2 leeks, cleaned and sliced
    into 5 cm (2 inch) strips
100 g (4 oz) new potatoes,
    scrubbed and sliced into
    5 mm ($^1/_4$ inch) discs
900 ml ($1^1/_2$ pints) stock
    or water
Sea salt and freshly ground
    black pepper
A few sprigs fresh thyme
2 boned, skinless chicken
    breasts
1 egg yolk
4 tablespoons single cream
2 tablespoons chopped fresh
    parsley

This soup is based on the Flemish dish waterzoi which is often made with fish as well as chicken.

Melt the butter in a large pan and add all the vegetables, stir well, and cook for 2–3 minutes. Add the stock or water, seasoning and thyme and simmer for a further 5 minutes.

Meanwhile cut the chicken into cubes. Add this to the pan and cook for a further 5 minutes, or until the chicken is cooked through. Beat the egg with the cream and, having taken the pan off the heat, add this mixture and the parsley to the soup. Stir and the soup should thicken slightly.

Serve at once in warmed soup bowls.

CHICKEN AND CHICK PEA SOUP

S E R V E S
—— 4 ——

This is a favourite store-cupboard soup. Simply add any green vegetable that's available. Instead of chicken you could use ham or smoked sausage.

Heat the oil in a large pan and fry the onion until transparent. Add the garlic, chicken meat and stir well. Now put in the carrots, chick peas, herbs, tomatoes and the stock or water. Add a little pepper and bring to the boil.

Simmer for 15 minutes, then taste and adjust the seasoning. Add the chosen green vegetable, cook for a further 2–3 minutes and serve.

INGREDIENTS

PREPARATION TIME
10 minutes
COOKING TIME
25 minutes

350 g (12 oz) boned,
  skinless chicken
1 onion, sliced
2 tablespoons olive oil
2 garlic cloves, crushed
2 carrots, peeled and sliced
1 × 400 g (14 oz) tin
  chick peas, drained
½ teaspoon freeze-dried
  mixed herbs
6–8 sun-dried tomato halves,
  sliced
1½ pints stock or water
Salt and freshly ground black
  pepper
Any fresh green vegetable
  (2 medium courgettes or a
  small handful of green
  beans or 100 g [4 oz]
  spinach), chopped

CHICKEN MULLIGATAWNY SOUP

SERVES

—— 6 ——

INGREDIENTS

PREPARATION TIME
15 minutes
COOKING TIME
30 minutes

1.2 litres (2 pints) water
175 g (6 oz) red lentils
1 large potato, peeled
    and diced
2 tablespoons oil
1 large onion, finely chopped
2 garlic cloves, crushed
2 tablespoons medium curry
    powder or to taste
1 large boned, skinless
    chicken breast
2.5 cm (1 inch) piece fresh
    ginger, peeled and grated
Salt and freshly ground black
    pepper
Natural yoghurt to serve
Chopped fresh coriander
    to serve

Mulligatawny soup originated in the days of the Raj. The British in India might have been prepared to make many sacrifices but they would not do without their comforting bowls of soup to start each meal.

Remember when cooking with lentils that old dried pulses will take much longer to cook so buy from a shop with a good turnover.

Bring the water to the boil in a large pan and add the lentils and potato. Simmer for 15 minutes. Meanwhile heat the oil in a frying-pan and cook the onion and garlic until they are just beginning to colour. Add the curry powder and stir and fry for 1 minute.

Chop the chicken breast and add to the frying-pan. Cook, stirring constantly, for another 2–3 minutes. Add the grated ginger and season with salt and pepper.

Pour the contents of the frying-pan into the pot with the potatoes and lentils and simmer for a further 15 minutes. Taste and adjust the seasoning. Mash the potatoes with the back of a spoon or a potato masher to break them down a little.

Serve in warm bowls topped with a spoonful of natural yoghurt and some chopped coriander leaves.

COLD SOUPS

O ne of my first memories of elegant dinner parties is of a bowl of chilled Vichysoisse. I remember that the soup was deliciously cool and refreshing and quite unlike anything I had tasted before. Vichysoisse is only one of a range of cold soups which fall into two categories: those that have been cooked and chilled and those that need no cooking.

There is both good news and bad news about the cooked soups. You do have to plan ahead, but then when you arrive home hot and hungry the meal is already half prepared.

Chilled yoghurt-based soups are very simple to make and would be ideal before a spicy meal. *Potato, Courgette and Tarragon Soup* (p. 110) makes excellent use of courgettes at the height of their summer season and I always look forward to a glut of ripe red tomatoes so as to make the *Tomato and Basil Soup* on page 111.

Garnish cold soups with chopped herbs, single cream and serve hot garlic bread along side.

CONTENTS

ROCKET AND LETTUCE SOUP

SERVES
—— 4 ——

L ettuce has a very light and delicate flavour so I am adding some rocket to give a sharper bite to this lettuce soup. Use a green lettuce like cos or little gem, rather than a crisp but tasteless lettuce such as iceberg!

Heat the oil in a large pan and fry the shallots until soft. Add the potatoes, some seasoning and the stock or water and simmer for 5 minutes. Add the lettuce and cook for a further 5 minutes. Now add most of the rocket leaves and cook for 2 minutes more.

Liquidize in small batches, adding the remaining rocket leaves to the last batch. Taste and adjust the seasoning and chill. Garnish with the parsley and serve with a dollop of crème fraîche or soured cream.

INGREDIENTS

PREPARATION TIME
15 minutes
COOKING TIME
20 minutes
CHILLING TIME
2 hours

1 tablespoon oil
2 shallots, finely chopped
2 medium potatoes, peeled
  and diced
Sea salt and freshly ground
  black pepper
600 ml (1 pint) stock
  or water
About 275 g (10 oz) green
  lettuce leaves, washed and
  shredded
A bunch of rocket leaves
Chopped fresh parsley
  to garnish
Crème fraîche or soured cream
  to serve

GAZPACHO

S E R V E S

—— 6 ——

INGREDIENTS

PREPARATION TIME
15 minutes

2 thick slices country-style
   white bread
3 tablespoons olive oil
2 tablespoons red wine
   vinegar
1–2 plump garlic cloves,
   crushed
Sea salt and freshly ground
   black pepper
1 large Spanish onion
$^1/_2$ cucumber, peeled
1 red pepper, de-seeded
1.2 litres (2 pints) chilled
   tomato juice
Ice cubes

This robustly flavoured soup was first made on farms in Spain. Using readily available ingredients and adding oil for extra nutrition it must have been an economical and refreshing drink.

This soup can be served with Crisp garlic croûtons (see p. 127).

Tear the bread into small pieces. With a wooden spoon, mix the oil and vinegar into the bread, then add the garlic, mashing everything together to make a paste. Season well.

Grate the vegetables (this can be done in a food processor) and stir into the bowl. Add the tomato juice and then taste and adjust the seasoning. Dilute the soup using ice-cubes.

Opposite: SPLIT PEA AND HAM SOUP *(Page 92)*
FIFTEEN-MINUTE CHEESE AND HERB SCONES *(Page 132)*

CREAM OF AVOCADO SOUP

S E R V E S
—— 4 ——

M ake this soup at the last moment. Be sure to scrape out all the dark green bits of avocado nearest the skin to ensure the soup has a lovely colour.

———

Peel the avocados and place the flesh in a food processor or blender. Add the tomato, onion and lemon juice and whiz until smooth.

Pour into a chilled bowl and season with salt, pepper and Tabasco.

Dilute to taste with iced water. Stir in some chopped parsley and serve.

INGREDIENTS

PREPARATION TIME
10 minutes

3 large ripe avocados
1 large tomato, peeled, de-
  seeded and roughly
  chopped
$^1/_4$ red onion
1 tablespoon lemon juice
  or to taste
Sea salt and freshly ground
  black pepper
A few drops of Tabasco
600 ml (1 pint) iced water
Fresh chopped parsley
  to garnish

Opposite: CRANBERRY CHRISTMAS SOUP *(Page 122)*
CREAM OF AVOCADO SOUP

GAZPACHO BLANCO

S E R V E S

—— 4 ——

PREPARATION TIME
15 minutes
CHILLING TIME
2 hours

75 g (3 oz) stale white bread,
crusts removed
600 ml (1 pint) water or
milk and water mixed
2 hard-boiled eggs
2 plump garlic cloves
75 g (3 oz) blanched whole
almonds
Sea salt and white pepper
150 ml (5 fl oz) extra virgin
olive oil
1–2 tablespoons white wine
vinegar
15 cm (6 inch) piece unpeeled
cucumber
300 ml (10 fl oz) ice cubes
(optional)
2 tablespoons chopped fresh
chives to garnish

A mong the chilled soups of Spain is this white gazpacho which has a base of almonds and mayonnaise.

Put the bread to soak in 150 ml (5 fl oz) of the water or milk and water mixture. Put the hard-boiled egg yolks, garlic, almonds, salt and pepper in a blender or food processor and process until you have a fine paste.

With the motor running, pour in the oil in a thin stream. Once all the oil has been added, put in the soaked bread. Now thin the soup with the remaining liquid, adding the vinegar to taste. Pour into a chilled serving bowl.

Chop the egg whites and finely dice the cucumber. Add these to the soup and then chill for 2 hours or stir in the ice cubes.

Serve scattered with chopped chives.

ICED TOMATO SOUP

SERVES
—— 6 ——

Similar in style to *Gazpacho* (p. 102), this soup is actually served frozen, Ideally you need an ice-cream churn to make it, but you could use a rigid container. Again, for speed you can use a food processor to grate the vegetables.

Break up the bread, then whiz in a food processor with the oil and vinegar.

Now add the remaining ingredients and process until well mixed. Season well, the mixture should be quite spicy at this stage.

Pour the mixture into the ice-cream churn and freeze until ready according to the manufacturer's instructions, or freeze in a rigid container in the coldest part of the freezer, beating from time to time. You may need to scrape down the sides of the churn from time to time as the mixture has a tendency to freeze unevenly.

Serve spooned into tall glasses garnished with a few leaves of fresh basil.

INGREDIENTS

PREPARATION TIME
10 minutes
FREEZING TIME
2–4 hours

2 slices fresh white bread,
  crusts removed
2 tablespoons olive oil
1 tablespoon wine vinegar
600 ml (1 pint) tomato juice
$^1/_2$ medium onion, grated
$^1/_2$ green pepper, de-seeded
  and finely grated
10 cm (4 inch) piece
  cucumber, peeled and
  grated
1 tablespoon vodka
A few drops of Tabasco
Sea salt and freshly ground
  black pepper
Basil leaves to garnish

WATERCRESS VICHYSSOISE

S E R V E S
—— 4 ——

Vichyssoise is the classic potato and leek soup that is most often served chilled. In this recipe I am replacing some of the leeks with watercress, thus combining two classic recipes to give a creamy, rich soup with a lovely peppery bite.

Heat the oil in a large pan and cook the shallots until soft. Now add the potatoes and leeks and stir well. Pour in the stock or water, season and simmer for 10 minutes.

Add the watercress and continue to cook for a further 2–3 minutes. Liquidize in small batches in a blender or food processor and then taste and adjust the seasoning. Remember that cold blunts flavour so add a little extra salt and pepper.

Chill for at least 2 hours, stir in the cream and serve garnished with the chopped chives.

INGREDIENTS

PREPARATION TIME
10 minutes
COOKING TIME
20 minutes
CHILLING TIME
2 hours

1 tablespoon oil
2 shallots, chopped
2 potatoes, peeled and diced
2 medium leeks, cleaned and
   finely sliced
900 ml (1½ pints) stock
   or water
Sea salt and freshly ground
   black pepper
A good bunch of green
   watercress, roughly chopped
150 ml (5 fl oz) single cream
1 tablespoon chopped fresh
   chives to garnish

GREEN PEA AND MINT SOUP

SERVES

—— 8 ——

Pea and mint soup is another lovely combination of summer flavours.

Heat the oil in a large pan and cook the onion until soft. Add the peas, chopped mint, sugar and some seasoning. Cook over a low heat for 2–3 minutes, then add half the stock, bring to the boil and simmer for 10 minutes.

Liquidize in small batches and then rub through a coarse sieve to remove the pea skins. Dilute with the remaining stock as necessary. Taste and adjust the seasoning.

Chill and serve topped with a spoonful of crème fraîche and garnish with a couple of tiny mint leaves.

INGREDIENTS

PREPARATION TIME
10 minutes
COOKING TIME
15 minutes
CHILLING TIME
2 hours

4 tablespoons olive oil
1 medium onion, chopped
900 g (2 lb) frozen petit pois
A bunch of fresh mint leaves,
    chopped
1 teaspoon sugar
Sea salt and black pepper
1.5 litres (2¹/₂ pints) chicken
    or vegetable stock
Crème fraîche to serve
Tiny mint leaves to garnish

POTATO, COURGETTE AND TARRAGON SOUP

SERVES
—— 4 ——

PREPARATION TIME
15 minutes
COOKING TIME
20 minutes
CHILLING TIME
2 hours

2 tablespoons olive oil
1 bunch spring onions,
  chopped
2 medium potatoes, peeled
  and diced
Sea salt and freshly ground
  black pepper
600 ml (1 pint) stock
  or water
4–6 small firm green
  courgettes
A bunch of fresh tarragon
  leaves
Lemon juice to taste
150 ml (5 fl oz) single cream
Tarragon leaves to garnish

This soup is a variation on the *Vichyssoise* on page 108. It uses small green courgettes and tarragon.

Heat the oil in a large pan and stir in the onions. Add the potatoes and cook for 2–3 minutes. Season and add the stock or water. Cook for 10 minutes.

Grate the courgettes, discarding any liquid that forms, and add them to the soup. Roughly chop the tarragon and add this too with some lemon juice to taste. Simmer for 2–3 minutes.

Liquidize in small batches. Stir in the cream. Adjust the seasoning and chill.

Serve garnished with a few tarragon leaves.

TOMATO AND BASIL SOUP

S E R V E S

—— 4 ——

Make this soup when tomatoes are at their most plentiful and most flavourful.

———

Roughly chop the tomatoes, reserving any juice that seeps out. In a large pan fry the shallots in the oil, then add the garlic, tomatoes, the stems from the basil leaves and a little seasoning. Cover the pan and cook for 5–10 minutes.

When the tomatoes are very soft and pulpy rub the mixture through a sieve. Return to a clean pan and add the sugar and stock or water. Cook for 2 minutes then taste and adjust the seasonings, adding vinegar to taste.

Chill and then stir in torn basil leaves.

INGREDIENTS

PREPARATION TIME
10 minutes
COOKING TIME
15 minutes
CHILLING TIME
2 hours

900 g (2 lb) fresh tomatoes
2 shallots, chopped
2 tablespoons olive oil
1 garlic clove, crushed
A good bunch of basil leaves
Salt and freshly ground black
    pepper
$^1/_2$ teaspoon sugar
600 ml (1 pint) vegetable
    stock or water
1 tablespoon wine vinegar

CUCUMBER AND YOGHURT SOUP

S E R V E S

—— 4 ——

PREPARATION TIME
10 minutes
COOKING TIME
5 minutes

1 tablespoon vegetable oil
1 teaspoon cumin seeds,
   lightly crushed
1 small onion, finely chopped
600 ml (1 pint) natural
   yoghurt
1 cucumber, peeled, de-seeded
   and grated
Sea salt and freshly ground
   black pepper
Iced water to taste
Chopped fresh coriander
   to garnish
Ground cumin to garnish

This spiced cucumber soup is based on the Indian drink lassi. If you have some good home-made chicken stock you could use it instead of water. Use a food processor to grate the cucumber in seconds.

Heat the oil in a frying-pan and cook the cumin seeds until they start to pop. Add the onion and fry until this is just beginning to colour. Cool.

Mix the cumin and onion with the yoghurt and add the grated cucumber, seasoning well.

Dilute the soup to taste with iced water and serve garnished with a little chopped fresh coriander and some ground cumin.

CARROT AND GINGER SOUP

S E R V E S

—— 4 ——

This is a rather unusual cold soup combining the sweetness of carrots with a spicy note of ginger.

———

Heat the oil in a large pan and cook the onion until soft. Add the garlic and ginger and stir well. Add the carrots and potato and cook for a further 2 minutes. Pour in the stock or water, season and simmer for 8–10 minutes or until the vegetables are soft.

Liquidize in small batches then taste and adjust the seasoning. Chill and garnish with chopped coriander and serve with crème fraîche.

INGREDIENTS

PREPARATION TIME
15 minutes
COOKING TIME
15 minutes
CHILLING TIME
2 hours

2 tablespoons oil
1 large onion, finely chopped
1 garlic clove, crushed
5 cm (2 inch) piece ginger,
    peeled and grated
1 large potato, peeled
    and diced
600 ml (1 pint) vegetable
    stock or water
Sea salt and freshly ground
    black pepper
Chopped fresh coriander
    leaves to garnish
Crème fraîche to serve

JELLIED CHICKEN CONSOMMÉ

SERVES

—— 4 ——

PREPARATION TIME
15 minutes
COOKING TIME
15 minutes
CHILLING TIME
2–4 hours

1.2 litres (2 pints) lightly
  jellied home made chicken
  stock
2 medium carrots
4 sticks of celery
2 small courgettes
2 tablespoons chopped fresh
  dill
Sea salt and freshly ground
  black pepper
Tabasco and lemon juice

TO SERVE
A few fronds of dill and
  flakes of Parmesan

This is a rather different summer soup, a semi-solid jelly filled with the tiniest dice of summer vegetables and chopped fresh herbs. You will need to use a home-made chicken stock for the soup to gel properly but that can be made in advance.

Remove as much fat as possible from the top of the chicken stock. Place in a large pan and bring to the boil.

Meanwhile peel the carrots, wash the celery and trim the courgettes. Cut the vegetables into thin strips, then into tiny dice.

Put the carrots and celery into the stock and simmer for 4–5 minutes. Remove any scum that rises to the surface. Add the courgettes, cook for a further minute then turn off the heat and stir in the dill.

Taste the soup. You will need to season it quite well as cold dulls flavour. Add the salt, pepper, Tabasco and lemon juice to taste. Pour into a bowl and chill.

When the soup is set lightly, stir to distribute the vegetables evenly, then spoon into dishes. Serve garnished with more herbs and some Parmesan flakes.

FRUIT SOUPS

Fruit soups are rather a novelty item on any menu except perhaps in Eastern Europe where they form an important part of a traditional love of soup. In Hungary there is even a saying that a meal is not a meal without a bowl of soup, so apricot, sour cherry and bilberry soups are commonly found on menus there.

The soups in this chapter are some that I've enjoyed, usually as a dessert course, for their unusual texture and flavour. While a dessert soup might seem a little strange at first, on further reflection it is a light and elegant way to finish a meal.

Summer fruits lend themselves particularly well to this idea giving a clean, fresh end to a meal on a hot August night and last Christmas I ate a lovely chilled cranberry soup that made a much more fitting finale to the festive meal than plum pudding.

Fruit soups are often served with a scoop of ice cream melting gently in the centre. Choose flavours to compliment the soup and serve crisp sweet biscuits alongside.

CONTENTS

RED FRUIT SOUP

S E R V E S
—— 6 ——

Known in our house as Soup of the Red Fruits, a literal translation of the French, this is a wonderful summer soup that can at a pinch be made with frozen fruit. Use a goodish red wine and for best results make it 24 hours before serving. In France a spoonful or two of fruit sorbet, blackcurrant or raspberry, is served in each bowl.

———

Place the wine in a large saucepan and, having washed the fruit and removed any leaves or stems, add it to the pan starting with the most resilient. So cherries and redcurrants first then on through blueberries, blackberries, logan- and tayberries and finishing with strawberries and raspberries.

Gently simmer each fruit for about 1 minute before adding the next. As soon as the strawberries and raspberries are in the pan switch off the heat.

Add sugar to taste, stirring gently to dissolve the crystals, then allow the soup to cool. Add the crème de cassis and chill until needed.

INGREDIENTS

PREPARATION TIME
10 minutes
COOKING TIME
5 minutes
CHILLING TIME
2 hours

¹/₂ bottle red wine (e.g. Cabernet Sauvignon)
1.25 kg (2¹/₂ lb) assorted red summer fruits (redcurrants, blueberries, blackberries, strawberries, raspberries, tayberries, loganberries, cherries)
175 g (6 oz) caster sugar or to taste
2 tablespoons crème de cassis

CHILLED MELON SOUP

S E R V E S
—— 4 ——

PREPARATION TIME
10 minutes
COOKING TIME
5 minutes

1 large or 2 medium ripe,
  perfumed melons
Lemon juice to taste
Chilled still mineral water
  to taste
A few mint leaves or edible
  flower petals to decorate

FOR THE SYRUP
250 ml (8 fl oz) water
100 g (4 oz) caster sugar

Melons are plentiful and fragrant just at that time in summer when you most need your thirst quenched, but the heat has robbed you of any trace of hunger. This soup is a marvellously refreshing one that could be served either side of the main course.

Make the syrup first. Place the water and sugar in a saucepan and bring to the boil, stirring to dissolve the sugar crystals. Simmer for 4 minutes. Cool.

Peel the melon and remove any pips. Cut into cubes and liquidize to a smooth purée. Add at least 1 tablespoon of lemon juice and sugar syrup to taste. If the purée is very thick you can thin it by adding a little chilled still mineral water.

Serve the soup in bowls decorated with a few mint leaves or edible summer flower petals.

BERRY AND YOGHURT SOUP

S E R V E S

—— 4 ——

This is an easy soup that looks very pretty and tastes rich and creamy.

Place the cleaned fruit in a serving bowl and mash gently with a fork. You don't want to break up the fruit too much, just allow the juices to run. Now sprinkle over the sugar and leave the fruit to macerate for 10 minutes.

Thin the yoghurt with the iced water then stir this into the bowl. Mix only until just combined. The soup should look a little streaky.

Sprinkle the top of the soup with cinnamon sugar. Serve at once.

INGREDIENTS

PREPARATION TIME
10 minutes + 10 minutes resting time

225 g (8 oz) small red fruit (e.g. raspberries, blueberries or redcurrants)
50 g (2 oz) caster sugar
600 ml (1 pint) natural yoghurt
About 150 ml (5 fl oz) iced water
Cinnamon sugar to decorate

MANGO RICE CREAM

SERVES
—— 4 ——

PREPARATION TIME
10 minutes
COOKING TIME
30 minutes
CHILLING TIME
2 hours

25 g (1 oz) sugar
40 g (1¹/₂ oz) ground rice
600 ml (1 pint) milk
2 medium very ripe fragrant
    mangoes
Lemon juice to taste

This recipe is based on one from Bombay where thin chilled fruit purées are served mixed into very thin milk puddings. As it has the consistency of soup I'm including it here.

Place the sugar, ground rice and milk into a heavy pan and simmer for about 20–30 minutes, stirring from time to time. You should have a mixture the consistency of double cream. Allow to cool.

Meanwhile, peel the mangoes, reserving about a quarter of the flesh. Purée the remaining fruit and stir this into the rice cream, taste and add lemon juice to sharpen the flavour if necessary.

Dice the reserved mango and add to the soup. Chill until needed.

STRAWBERRY SOUP WITH STRAWBERRY YOGURT ICE

SERVES

—— 4 ——

Strawberries, very red and ripe, are a traditional summer delight. Use the reddest, ripest and most perfumed you can find for this dish.

———————

Start with the syrup. Place the water and 100 g (4 oz) sugar in a heavy-bottomed saucepan and bring to the boil, stirring to dissolve the sugar crystals. Simmer for 4–5 minutes.

Liquidize the strawberries and if the pips worry you rub through a sieve to remove them. Add enough cooled syrup to dilute and sweeten to taste; then chill.

Meanwhile purée the remaining berries with icing sugar to taste and the yoghurt. The mixture should be quite sweet. Freeze either in an ice-cream churn or in a tray, beating with a fork once or twice to give a smooth ice.

Serve the purée in shallow bowls with a spoonful of softish ice in the centre of each dish.

INGREDIENTS

PREPARATION TIME
15 minutes
COOKING TIME
5 minutes
FREEZING TIME
4 hours

750 g (1¹/₂ lb) ripe strawberries

FOR THE SYRUP
250 ml (8 fl oz) water
100 g (4 oz) caster sugar plus extra to taste

FOR THE ICE
450 g (1 lb) ripe strawberries
Icing sugar to taste
300 ml (10 fl oz) Greek yoghurt

CRANBERRY CHRISTMAS SOUP

SERVES
—— 4 ——

Judging a cranberry competition, I was asked what unusual ideas I might have for cranberries. I had to admit they were not something I thought of often but when trying out various recipes in the kitchen I made this soup and was very pleased with its rich colour and lovely flavour. Serve the soup with a spoonful of quite soft, good quality vanilla ice melting gently in the centre of each bowl.

Place the cranberries and water into a saucepan and simmer over a low heat until the fruit is very soft. Rub the mixture through a sieve into a bowl.

Meanwhile make the syrup. Heat the water and sugar in a saucepan, stirring until the sugar has dissolved. Add the cinnamon and simmer for 3–4 minutes. Add to the cranberry mixture. Chill and serve as above.

INGREDIENTS

PREPARATION TIME
10 minutes
COOKING TIME
10 minutes
CHILLING TIME
2 hours

---

450 g (1 lb) fresh or frozen cranberries
600 ml (1 pint) water
FOR THE SYRUP
250 ml (8 fl oz) water
100 g (4 oz) caster sugar
1 teaspoon ground cinnamon

PEACH NECTAR

SERVES
—— 4 ——

Perfect when peaches are plentiful, this thick uncooked purée is garnished with a contrasting summer fruit.

Place the peaches in a large bowl and cover with boiling water. After 2–3 minutes the skins should slip off easily.

Put the peach flesh, minus the stones, in a blender liquidizer with the caster sugar and lemon juice. Process until smooth. Pour the purée into 4 shallow dishes.

Now make a raspberry coulis by rubbing the raspberries through a sieve and sweetening them with a little icing sugar. Just before serving pour a swirl of coulis into each bowl of peach purée.

INGREDIENTS

PREPARATION TIME
15 minutes

4–5 large ripe peaches
50 g (2 oz) caster sugar
A good squeeze of lemon juice
225 g (8 oz) fresh raspberries
Icing sugar to taste

Apple and Cinnamon Soup

S E R V E S

—— 4 ——

Use apples that give a very soft purée, such as Bramleys, and sharpen the flavour with lemon or orange juice.

———

Place the apples and 300 ml (10 fl oz) water in a saucepan and bring to the boil. Simmer until you have a soft purée.

Add juice and sugar to taste, stirring them into the hot purée. Now add the cinnamon and allow to cool.

Dilute the purée a little with iced water. The soup should be quite thick. Serve sprinkled with crushed amaretti biscuits.

INGREDIENTS

PREPARATION TIME
15 minutes
COOKING TIME
10 minutes

450 g (1 lb) apples, peeled,
cored and sliced
300 ml (10 fl oz) water
1 tablespoon lemon
or orange juice
Caster sugar to taste
1 teaspoon ground cinnamon
300 ml (10 fl oz) iced water
or to taste
2 or 3 amaretti biscuits,
roughly crushed, to decorate

CHILLED APRICOT SOUP

S E R V E S
—— 6 ——

PREPARATION TIME
15 minutes
COOKING TIME
25 minutes
CHILLING TIME
(OPTIONAL)
2 hours

225 g (8 oz) dried apricots
200 ml (7 fl oz) white wine
1.5 litres (2¹/₂ pints) water
2 tablespoons white
* breadcrumbs*
3 tablespoons caster sugar
1 egg yolk
150 ml (5 fl oz) soured
* cream*
Lemon juice to taste

A Hungarian soup this, so it is an authentic Eastern European dish. Either soak the dried apricots overnight or use the very soft 'ready-to-eat' ones.

———

If necessary soak the apricots overnight. Chop the fruit into small pieces and simmer half in the wine for 20 minutes.

At the same time simmer the remaining apricots in about 900 ml (1¹/₂ pints) of water with the breadcrumbs until soft, about 20 minutes.

Liquidize the apricot/breadcrumb mixture, return to a saucepan and mix in the sugar and the apricot and wine mixture. Bring to the boil (if very thick dilute with the remaining water) and remove from the heat.

In a warmed soup tureen mix the egg yolk and soured cream. Pour on the boiling soup, beating well. Add lemon juice to taste.

Serve hot or well chilled.

GARNISHES

By adding the right garnish a simple soup can be turned into something even more splendid. Crunchy croûtons add taste and texture. *Herb-spiked crème fraîche* (p. 128) adds richness.

Many of the garnishes given in this chapter may be made ahead, stored in the appropriate fashion, then re-heated if necessary when they are needed.

Choose a garnish considering the other flavours of the soup. It would be unfortunate to garnish with dill if the main taste sensation is of coriander. Add crisp garnishes at the last moment or hand round separately after the soup has been served.

For last minute garnishes, try single cream, crumbled crackers, crisp fried bacon bits, grated cheese, chopped olives and herbs, or a spoonful of a ready-made sauce like pesto.

CONTENTS

CRISP GARLIC CROÛTONS

SERVES

—— 4 ——

Possibly my favourite garnish and one that can be very rich. Use a well-flavoured oil and keep the temperature of the pan quite hot to prevent the bread becoming fat logged and soggy.

INGREDIENTS

PREPARATION TIME
5 minutes
COOKING TIME
5 minutes

Slice the bread into cubes about 1–inch square

Heat the oil in a large frying pan and when hot add the bread and crushed garlic. Fry until golden on all sides, you may need to add a little extra oil depending on the absorbency of the bread. Carefully turn the croûtons, cooking until they are golden brown on all sides.

If using garlic salt add it to taste at this stage.

Drain on absorbent paper and serve hot with most soups.

3–4 slices day old bread
(white or brown)
3–4 tablespoons olive oil
1 plump garlic clove, crushed
or 1 teaspoon garlic salt

CHEESE CROÛTONS

SERVES

—— 4 ——

Adding cheese croûtons to soup can liven up even the most mundane tin of tomato.

INGREDIENTS

2 slices white bread
2-3 tablespoons olive oil
2 tablespoons freshly grated
Parmesan

Pre-heat the oven to 220°C/400°F/Gas 6. Brush both sides of the bread generously with olive oil and sprinkle with Parmesan on one side. Cut into 2.5 cm (1 inch) squares, place on a baking sheet and cook in the oven for 10-15 minutes.

HERB-SPIKED CRÈME FRAÎCHE

SERVES
—— 4 ——

INGREDIENTS

PREPARATION TIME
5 minutes

100 g (4 oz) crème fraîche
2–3 tablespoons choppd fresh
   herbs (tarragon, dill,
   summer savoury and
   coriander are all excellent)
1 large fresh garlic clove,
   finely crushed
Sea salt and freshly ground
   black pepper

This is a good way to enrich a soup whose flavour may seem a little thin. Excellent with fresh summer vegetable soups, this creamy mixture can be made with whatever fresh herbs you have to hand. If you don't love garlic try substituting a spoonful of chopped chives.

Mix everything together well adjusting the seasoning according to personal taste.

Serve a spoonful of the garnish in bowls of hot or cold soup.

GARLIC BREAD

S E R V E S

—— 4–6 ——

Once in a while I love hot garlic bread. Eaten straight from the oven, dripping in butter this recipe is not for the faint hearted.

———

Pre-heat the oven to 200°C/400°F/Gas 6.

Cut the loaf in half.

Slice the two halves into ¹/₂-inch sections making sure you stop just before the bottom crust.

Melt the butter in a small saucepan and add the garlic, parsley and a little seasoning.

Cut two sheets of foil large enough to hold the bread. Place a piece of bread on each sheet of foil then pour on the butter making sure it seeps down between all the cut edges. Fold over the foil and crimp the edges.

Bake the bread in the pre-heated oven for 10–15 minutes opening the foil for the last few minutes to crisp the tops of the loaves.

Serve at once.

INGREDIENTS

PREPARATION TIME
5–10 minutes
COOKING TIME
10–15 minutes

1 loaf of French bread

100 g (4 oz) butter

2 plump garlic cloves peeled and crushed

2 tablespoons chopped fresh parsley

Sea salt and pepper

CHILLI AND TOMATO SALSA

MAKES

—— 200 ml (7 fl oz) ——

A spoonful of this piquant tomato salsa is delicious added to bean soups.

PREPARATION TIME
15 minutes

3 tomatoes
1 medium onion
1–2 green chillies
2 tablespoons fresh parsley or
   fresh coriander, roughly
   chopped
A squeeze of lemon juice
Sea salt and freshly ground
   black pepper

Place the tomatoes in a bowl and cover with boiling water. Leave for 2–3 minutes then slip off the skins. Slice open and spoon out and discard the seeds.

Peel and quarter the onion.

Carefully de-seed the chilli and chop roughly.

Place these ingredients in a food processor with the parsley or coriander and whiz for a few seconds until the relish is finely chopped.

Spoon into a bowl and season to taste with the salt, pepper and lemon juice.

Allow the relish to sit for a few minutes before serving.

TOASTED PITTA TRIANGLES

S E R V E S

—— 4 ——

If you cut these triangles very small you could serve them in the soup. I like to serve them, hot from the oven, alongside.

———

Pre-heat the oven to 200°C/400°F/Gas 6.

Cut the pitta breads open and brush with the oil. Slice into triangles and place on a baking sheet. Sprinkle on the Parmesan in an even layer.

Just before serving, bake the triangles in the pre-heated oven for 8–12 minutes or until golden brown.

Serve at once.

INGREDIENTS

PREPARATION TIME
5 minutes
COOKING TIME
12 minutes

*2 large sized pitta breads
(white or brown)*
2 tablespoons olive oil
*2 tablespoons freshly grated
Parmesan*

FIFTEEN-MINUTE CHEESE AND HERB SCONES

MAKES
—— 8–10 ——

PREPARATION TIME
5 minutes
COOKING TIME
10–12 minutes

250 g (9 oz) plain flour
2 level teaspoons baking
  powder
¹/₄ teaspoon salt
1 teaspoon dried mixed herbs
50 g (2 oz) grated cheddar
5 tablespoons vegetable oil
150 ml (5 fl oz) milk

These scones are simple to make and can bake in the oven while the soup simmers.

Pre-heat the oven to 230°C/450°F/Gas 8.

Mix the dry ingredients and the cheese in a bowl then add the oil and milk mixing to a smooth dough.

Turn onto a lightly floured board and knead lightly.

Press or roll out to 1.5 cm (³/₄ inch) thick then cut into 8-10 scones.

Place on a baking sheet, brush the tops with milk and bake in the pre-heated oven for 10–12 minutes or until well risen and golden brown.

MELBA TOAST

M A K E S

—— 12 slices ——

This is a wonderful old fashioned recipe that my whole family loves.

PREPARATION TIME
5 minutes
COOKING TIME
10–20 minutes

Pre-heat the oven to 200°C/400°F/Gas 6.

Toast the bread on both sides until lightly coloured.

Cut the crusts from the bread then cut right through the centre to give two thin slices.

Place the slices on a baking sheet and cook in the pre-heated oven for 10–20 minutes or until golden brown. Cool and store in an air tight tin until needed.

6 slices day old white bread

INDEX

Entries in *italic* refer to illustrations